We Ha~
Guardian

Some Instances
of Divine Intervention
in British History

COMPILED BY

W. B. GRANT

WITH NEW MATERIAL BY

MICHAEL A. CLARK

THE COVENANT PUBLISHING CO. LTD.
121, Low Etherley, Bishop Auckland, Co. Durham, DL14 0HA

2011

Fourth Edition - revised and enlarged 1952
New Impression 1957
Reprinted 1972
Reprinted 1976
Reprinted 1989
Reprinted 1996
Fifth Edition – revised and enlarged 2011

ISBN 978-085205-104-7

Printed by
THE COVENANT PUBLISHING COMPANY LIMITED
121, Low Etherley, Bishop Auckland,
Co. Durham, DL14 0HA
www.covpub.co.uk

WILLIAM BROOKE GRANT
1903 – 1984

W. B. Grant had a long association with the B. I. Movement extending over fifty years. He was an Editor of *The National Message* and a Member of the Board of Management of the British-Israel-World Federation.

During the early 1930s he was engaged in his professional career as a Chartered Mechanical Engineer, working in the Plymouth and South Western Area, including the Cornish Tin Mines. At this time he was on the Committee of the Plymouth Branch of the BIWF, later joining the Harrow Weald Bible College. Following his course of training, he was appointed Personal Assistant to Dr. W. Pascoe Goard in 1935. From this time he became increasingly involved in vital affairs at B. I. Headquarters at 6 Buckingham Gate, London, especially so as, later, the Second World War of 1939-45 increased in fearful intensity.

Reference to his many writings in *The National Message* and related publications of those incredible years will provide proof of his devotion to the Bible and Christian Faith. His book *We Have a Guardian* was first published in 1944 by Covenant Publishing. This is the Fifth Edition and it continues to inspire and comfort his readers.

He that dwelleth in the secret place of the most High shall abide
under the shadow of the Almighty.
I will say of the LORD, He is my refuge and my fortress: my
God; in him will I trust.
Surely he shall deliver thee from the snare of the fowler, and
from the noisome pestilence.
He shall cover thee with his feathers, and under his wings shalt
thou trust: his truth shall be thy shield and buckler.
Thou shalt not be afraid for the terror by night; nor for the
arrow that flieth by day;
Nor for the pestilence that walketh in darkness; nor for the
destruction that wasteth at noonday.
A thousand shall fall at thy side, and ten thousand at thy right
hand; but it shall not come nigh thee.

PSALM 91:1-7

'No weapon . . . shall prosper'

This book, three editions of which were published during the later years of World War II, was compiled with the object of making known some of the numerous forthright statements by British Cabinet Ministers, Clergy, Senior Officers of the Fighting Services, Journalists and others at various critical stages during the great conflict. They expressed their profound conviction that Divine Intervention was vouchsafed on behalf of the Armed Forces of Britain, Australia, Canada, New Zealand, South Africa, the United States and our Allies fighting for freedom against the forces of evil and oppression.

Since 1945, much additional evidence became available and the fourth edition was a greatly enlarged version of the former work. A number of further testimonies were included and the background of many operations was filled in from official documents and memoirs. The evidence that God intervened and gave us victory, despite our mistakes and folly, is overwhelming. This fifth edition has added sections about events from more recent decades.

The significant fact also emerges that Commanding Officers believed and Padres taught that we were the servants of God in the cause of justice, liberty, freedom and peace. May we not believe that the promise of the Lord made through His prophet Isaiah was fulfilled? This was that *"No weapon that is formed against thee shall prosper . . . this is the heritage of the servants of the Lord, and their righteousness is of Me"* (*Isaiah* 54:17).

Since those days, to our great loss, we have turned our backs on God. We have sought a secular Utopia instead of heeding Christ's injunction: *'Seek ye first the kingdom of God, and His righteousness'* (*Matthew* 6:25-34). What a sorry plight we are in today! Dare we expect God to deliver us from our present rejection of His Law and use us again as His servants – a *'company of nations'* guided by His Divine Will?

As individuals making up our nation, we have a unique responsibility in this matter. This is true whether we be subjects of Her Majesty at home or abroad, citizens of the United States of America or of the freedom-loving countries of North-West Europe. Do we acknowledge our need for and dependence upon Almighty God? Do we ask that Christ shall rule our lives and direct our national affairs that we might lead the nations in peace?

We Have a Guardian

An affirmation of profound significance to the people of Britain, and indeed to all the peoples of the British Commonwealth and the United States, was made by Mr. Winston Churchill when he addressed three thousand mine-owners' and mine-workers' delegates on October 31, 1942. In the course of his speech the Prime Minister said:

'I sometimes have a feeling of interference. I want to stress that. I have a feeling sometimes that some Guiding Hand has interfered. I have a feeling that we have a Guardian because we have a great Cause, and we shall have that Guardian so long as we serve that Cause faithfully. And what a Cause it is!'

Mr. Churchill's faith was vindicated to the full by event after event during World War II. Moreover, the history of the English-speaking people abounds with deliverances which can be accounted for in no other way than as acts of Divine Intervention.

The Spanish Armada

Philip of Spain, realizing that only the English stood in the way of the security of his dominions in the New World and his supremacy in Europe, determined to conquer England. To this end, he assembled what he thought to be the Invincible Armada. On July 19, 1588, the sails of the Armada were sighted, and as it swept in a broad crescent past Plymouth, moving towards its point of junction with Philip's invasion forces waiting at Calais, the English fleet under Lord Howard of Effingham gave chase. John Richard Green, the historian, states:

'In numbers the two forces were strangely unequal; the English fleet counted only 80 vessels against the 149 which composed the Armada. In size of ships the disproportion was even greater. Fifty of the English vessels, including the squadron of the Lord Admiral and the craft of the volunteers, were little bigger than yachts of the present day. Even of the thirty Queen's ships which formed its main body, there were only four which equalled in tonnage the smallest of the Spanish galleons. . . . Small however as the English ships were, they were in perfect trim; they sailed two feet for the Spaniards' one, and their Admiral was backed by a crowd of captains who had won fame in the Spanish seas. With him was Hawkins, who had been the first to break into the charmed circle of the Indies; Frobisher, the hero of the North-West passage; and above all Drake, who held command of the privateers. . . .

'Closing in or drawing off as they would, the lightly-handled English vessels, which fired four shots to the Spaniards' one, hung boldly on the rear of the great fleet as it moved along the Channel. Now halting, now moving slowly on, the running fight between the two fleets lasted throughout the week, till the Armada dropped anchor in Calais roads' (*A Short History of the English People,* 1891 edn., p. 418).

The time had now come for sharper work if the junction of the Armada with the invasion army was to be prevented; for the Spaniards' loss in ships had not been great. Howard decided to force an engagement and, lighting eight fire-ships, sent them down with the tide upon the Spanish line. The galleons at once cut their cables and stood out in panic to sea. Drake resolved at all costs to prevent their return, and at dawn the English ships closed in, and almost their last cartridge was spent ere the sun went down. Three great galleons had sunk, three had drifted helplessly on to the Flemish coast; but the bulk of the Spanish vessels remained.

The work of destruction, however, had been left to a mightier foe than Drake. Supplies fell short and the English vessels were obliged to give up the chase but the Spanish were quite unable to re-form, their last chance to do so being destroyed by a gale. The wind was so violently against them that they were forced to steer in a circuit around the British Isles, and on this journey to their home port many of the already damaged and battered vessels were driven ashore on the coasts of Scotland and Ireland. Only fifty vessels reached Corunna, carrying a few thousand men stricken with pestilence and death. So failed Philip's plan for the invasion of England and with it his dream of world domination.

In commemoration of this great deliverance Queen Elizabeth ordered and had struck gold and silver medals. The silver medal bears the inscription, 'He blew, and they were scattered,' and above that inscription is the name 'Jehovah' in Hebrew. On the obverse side is depicted a church founded upon a rock, together with the inscription, in Latin, 'I am assailed, but not injured.'

Invasion Twice Foiled

In 1759 Hawke, who was watching the French fleet at Brest lest it should sail to join the troop transports assembled to carry out the projected invasion of England, reported: 'While the wind is fair for the enemy's coming out, it is also favourable for our keeping them in, and when we are obliged to keep off they cannot stir.' Later, the British withdrawing momentarily for fresh supplies, the French fleet left Brest only to be pursued to Quiberon Bay, where it was attacked and destroyed in a heavy gale.

Napoleon too resolved to conquer England. 'Fifteen millions of people,' he said, in allusion to the disproportion between the population of England and France, 'must give way to forty millions.' And setting difficulties contemptuously aside, an invasion of England was planned on a gigantic scale. A camp of one hundred thousand men was formed at Boulogne, and a host of flat-bottomed boats gathered for their conveyance across the Channel. 'Let us be masters of the Channel for six hours,' Napoleon declared, 'and we are masters of the world.'

However, the skilfully combined plan, by which the British fleet would have been divided while the whole French Navy was concentrated in the Channel, was delayed by the death of the Admiral chosen to execute it. Then, on October 21, 1805, Nelson gained his glorious victory at Trafalgar which finally shattered Napoleon's schemes for invasion.

Ten years later it was through the power of British Arms, fighting with their Allies and helped by timely rain, that Napoleon's career was ended at Waterloo. 'If it had not rained the night between 17th and 18th of June,' wrote Victor Hugo, 'the future of Europe would have been changed.'

The Angels of Mons

In the early months of World War I the 'contemptible little British Army'—as the German High Command termed it—was hurriedly equipped and sent across the Channel to support the French and Belgian Allies; but these combined forces were far weaker in guns and man power than the Germans, and so, fighting a dogged rearguard action, they fell back before the terrific impact of massed enemy attacks. Serious defeat and tremendous losses appeared inevitable; but, during two days' fighting around Mons, the German advance was halted long enough to allow the British Expeditionary Force to withdraw.

Much has been written on the subject of the Angels of Mons and there have been many versions of the phenomena, but it is not inconsistent to believe that they were all substantially true though they differed in certain aspects. A number of accounts are gathered together and examined by Harold Begbie in his book, *On the Side of the Angels,* and few readers will remain unconvinced that both British and German troops were aware of supra-natural intervention during the battle.

The White Cavalry

In the spring of 1918 the Germans broke through the Allied Line. Heavy casualties were sustained, reserves were practically exhausted, and the Americans were not quite ready. Describing how the German advance was checked, an article in the journal of the Brigade of Guards (*Household Brigade Magazine*—Winter, 1942), states:

'At the focal point of the enemy's advance, Bethune, the Germans concentrated high explosive and machine-gun fire, preparatory to bayonet attack in mass formation. Suddenly the enemy shell fire lifted and concentrated on a slight rise beyond the town. The ground here was absolutely bare—yet enemy machine guns and shells raked it from end to end with a hail of lead.

'As suddenly as it started, the enemy's fire ceased, and in the complete silence there rose a lark's trilling song of thankfulness. The dense line of German troops which had started to move forward to victory in mass formation halted dead. And as the British watched, they saw it break! The Germans threw down everything they had—and fled in frantic panic. And here is the statement of a senior German officer who was taken prisoner immediately afterwards:

'The order had been given to advance in mass formation, and our troops were marching behind us singing their way to victory when Fritz, my lieutenant here, said: "Herr Kapitan, just look at that open ground behind Bethune, there is a Brigade of Cavalry coming up through the smoke drifting across it. They must be mad, these English, to advance against such a force as ours in the open. I suppose they must be cavalry of one of their Colonial Forces, for, see, they are all in white uniform and are mounted on white horses."

' "Strange," I said, "I have never heard of the English having any white-uniformed cavalry, whether Colonial or not. They have all been fighting on foot for several years past, and anyway they are in khaki, not white."

' "Well, they are plain enough," he replied. "See, our guns have got their range now; they will be blown to pieces in no time."

'We saw the shells bursting among the horses and their riders, all of whom came forward at a quiet walk-trot, in parade-ground formation, each man and horse in his exact place.

'Shortly afterwards our machine-guns opened a heavy fire, raking the advancing cavalry with a hail of lead; but on they came and not a single man or horse fell.

'Steadily they advanced, clear in the shining sunlight; and a few paces in front of them rode their leader, a fine figure of a man, whose hair, like spun gold, shone in an aura around his head. By his side was a great sword, but his hands lay quietly holding the reins, as his huge white charger bore him proudly forward.

'In spite of heavy shell and concentrated machine-gun fire the White Cavalry advanced, remorseless as fate, like the incoming tide surging over a sandy beach. . . .

'Then a great fear fell on me, and I turned to flee; yes, I, an officer of the Prussian Guard, fled, panic stricken, and around me were hundreds of terrified men, whimpering like children, throwing away their arms and accoutrements in order not to have their movements impeded. . . all running.

'Their one desire was to get away from that advancing White Cavalry; above all from their awe-inspiring leader whose hair shone like a golden aureole.

'That is all I have to tell you. We are beaten. The German Army is broken. There may be fighting, but we have lost the war; we are beaten—by the White Cavalry . . . I cannot understand . . . I cannot understand.

'(*Taken from the account of the Staff Captain, 1st Corps Intelligence, 1st British Army Headquarters, 1916-18, who was present and himself took the above statement from the German officer.)*

'During the days that followed, many German prisoners were examined and their accounts tallied in substance with the one given here.'

Zeppelin Tactics and the Weather

Another 1914-18 War incident is of interest: the Germans planned greatly to extend their air offensive, and it was intended to use Zeppelins which were to drift silently with the wind, their engines being cut out, across the target. The first raid trying out these new tactics was made on October 19, 1917. The Meteorological Correspondent of *The Observer* (17.10.37), drawing attention to the twentieth anniversary of this raid, wrote:

'Towards moonset on the evening of October 19, 1917, a fleet of eleven Zeppelins left Germany in what were thought to be ideal conditions for an attack on London—light westerly breezes, clear skies, and a low-lying mist. Guided by the then novel method of radio direction-finding, nine of the aircraft reached the Metropolis, one passing over the West End and dropping a bomb in Piccadilly.

'Meantime, an unforeseen cyclonic disturbance was forming off our south-west coast. While the ground mist thickened into fog, obliterating landmarks, the upper wind veered northward, and rapidly freshened from twenty to over fifty miles an hour at the invaders' height of 15,000 to 20,000 feet. The Zeppelins' directional radio apparatus failed, owing, it was believed, to the sudden intense cold, and, as a result, the raiders completely lost their bearings. All unawares, they were driven southward far off their homeward course.

'During the small hours of October 20, reckoning that they should be over Holland, the navigating officers ordered a descent to lower levels in the hope of recognizing their position. Actually, they found themselves over France, well behind the enemy lines. Several of the Zeppelins were promptly shot down; one escaped south-westward, but fell into the sea; and, to cap the disaster, the "flagship" of the fleet came down intact into the hands of the French.'

Lt. Col. Sir Alfred Rawlinson, C.M.G., C.B.E., D.S.O., who was actively connected with the defence of London, declared: 'On that night London was once more defended by "Powers" which were beyond the control of the defence. . . . Our faithful and invaluable ally the wind continued to "freshen" with most persistent and truly gratifying regularity' (*The Defence of London, 1915-18*, p. 218).

The National Day of Prayer, August 4, 1918
Again and again there has been unmistakable evidence of direct answers to National Days of Prayer, especially so when it is truly representative

through the Sovereign, as head of Church and State, together with the Ministers of the Crown and both Houses of Parliament. The following are extracts from an article entitled 'Calling the Nation to Prayer,' in *The National Message* dated September 13, 1939:

'On August 4, 1918—the fourth Anniversary of Britain's declaration of war against Germany—special services of thanksgiving and intercession were held all over the country. It was by no means the first time during the Great War that services of intercession were held throughout the British Isles. But this occasion was unique in that it was formally led by King George V, with both Houses of Parliament, at St. Margaret's, Westminster. Indeed, it proved to be an unprecedented Act of State, which had the most miraculous results.

'To appreciate the full significance of what followed it is necessary to recall that in March, 1918, the British Army had suffered a serious reverse in the breakthrough of the Germans at the part of the line held by the Fifth Army, and the months which immediately followed this disaster represented a period during which the war morale of the British people was at its lowest ebb. Now comes the National Day of Prayer, August 4, 1918, and it is only necessary to search through the pages of *The Times*—or any of the other national dailies—to see the miraculous way in which the tide was turned from that date and the Allied Cause was swept on to victory.

'An Allied attack began on August 8, commencing an advance which never ceased until the Armistice was signed on November 11, 1918. *The Times'* special correspondent described the new offensive as a brilliant success, and declared: "Victory was in the air."

'On August 10 *The Times'* headlines read: "The New Allied Offensive. Prisoners Seventeen Thousand." The leading article declared: "The new offensive initiated under the command of Sir Douglas Haig is one of the greatest and most gratifying surprises of the war. Even the weather favoured the Allies, for the assault was launched under cover of a thick mist. No offensive in which the British Army has participated has ever made so much progress on the opening day." Reports received from German sources confirmed the significance of this remarkable and surprising change of fortune in the complaint that "the Allies were favoured by a thick fog."

'It is not necessary to search the papers beyond August 31, when *The Times'* leader summarised the events of the previous twenty-one days by saying: "During the last day or two the pace of the German retreat on the Western front has been accelerated, and this is a good sign. Armies claiming to retire by their own choice do not hurry back as the Germans have been doing."

'Here was the great advance fully launched in a flowing tide which swept all before it until the armies heard the call "Cease Fire!" on Armistice Day. Surely it was more than mere coincidence that depression was turned into triumph immediately following the National Day of Prayer. Victory was in the air from that day and forward.'

The Commonwealth at Prayer, May 26, 1940

Twenty-two years after the victory which followed the National Day of Prayer on August 4, 1918, the British Army was in mortal peril. On May 10, 1940, the Germans launched the Blitzkrieg against the Low Countries and France. By the end of the second week in May the French defences at Sedan and on the Meuse were broken and there followed the rapid advance of German Panzer forces across France and Belgium. King Leopold capitulated, the Belgian Army ceased to resist, and the German 'armoured scythe-stroke almost reached Dunkirk,' the only port from which to evacuate the British Expeditionary Force. On May 27, the German High Command went so far as to boast: 'The British Army is encircled, our troops are proceeding to its annihilation.' The position was serious beyond measure. Afterwards, in a speech in the House of Commons on June 4, Mr. Churchill revealed how grave had been the prospect:

'When a week ago today I asked the House to fix this afternoon as the occasion for a statement, I feared it would be my hard lot to announce the greatest military disaster in our long history. I thought—and some good judges agreed with me—that perhaps 20,000 or 30,000 men might be re-embarked. . . . The whole root and core and brain of the British Army, on which and around which we were to build, and are to build, the great British Armies in the later years of the war, seemed about to perish upon the field, or to be led into ignominious and starving captivity.'

Meanwhile, at the request of King George VI, a National Day of Prayer was held on May 26. In an inspiring broadcast, His Majesty called the people of Britain and the Empire to commit their cause to God. Together with members of the Cabinet the King attended Westminster Abbey, whilst millions of his subjects in all parts of the Commonwealth and Empire flocked to the churches to join in prayer. The *Daily Sketch* of the following morning exclaimed: 'Nothing like it has ever happened before.'

The Miracle of Dunkirk

Soon the word 'miracle' was heard on all sides—the impossible had happened: 335,000 men had been carried 'out of the jaws of death and shame to their native land.' In his speech of June 4, Mr. Churchill referred to 'a miracle of deliverance, achieved by valour, by perseverance, by perfect discipline, by faultless service, by resource, by skill, by unconquerable fidelity.' But even so, this deliverance would have been impossible had it not been aided by two wonders—violent storm and Channel calm.

Sunday, June 9, was appointed as a Day of National Thanksgiving, and the following extracts from an article by C.B. Mortlock in *The Daily Telegraph* of June 8, bear striking testimony 'that the prayers of the nation were answered and that the God of Hosts Himself supported the valiant men of the British Expeditionary Force':

'Piece by piece the epic story of the great deliverance of the B.E.F. from the hands of the enemy is being unfolded.

'As the story is told, two great wonders stand forth; and on them have turned the fortune of the troops.

'I have talked to officers and men who have got safely back to England, and all of them tell of these two phenomena. The first was the great storm which broke over Flanders on Tuesday, May 28, and the other was the great calm which settled on the English Channel during the days following.

'Officers of high rank do not hesitate to put down the deliverance of the B.E.F. to the fact of the nation being at prayer on Sunday, May 26. . . . The consciousness of miraculous deliverance pervades the camps in which the troops are now housed in England. An instance of that occurred soon after a large camp had been more or less improvised, and many willing helpers were rivalling each other in giving comfort, refreshment and entertainment to the men. Among other arrangements was an E.N.S.A. concert, and, in the midst of it, at the request of the men, the chaplain conducted an act of thanksgiving consisting of a hymn and prayers and a few simple words.

'One chaplain told me that he was in a party who were taken aboard a minesweeper. They were all drenched to the skin, having been up to the shoulders in water. On deck it was impossible for anybody to stand. Presently there was a call for the padre to say a prayer. With the help of men on either side of him and behind him, the chaplain got up and the whole of the bedraggled ship's company joined with him in offering thanksgiving to God for their wonderful deliverance.

'The story of the strange armada which took the men from the beaches of Dunkirk is already familiar in outline. In its complete fulness it will probably never be known, but it is undoubted that there was such a calmness over the whole of the waters of the English Channel for that vital period of days as has rarely been experienced. Those who are accustomed to the Channel testify to the strangeness of this calm; they are deeply impressed by the phenomenon of Nature by which it became possible for tiny craft to go back and forth in safety.

'So the two miracles made possible what seemed impossible. In the darkness of the storm and the violence of the rain, formations which were eight to twelve miles from Dunkirk were able to move up on foot to the coast with scarcely any interruption from aircraft, for aircraft were unable to operate in such turbulent conditions.

'Chaplains have remarked on another circumstance that seems almost miraculous—the strange immunity by which the troops at times were favoured. One of them told me, for instance, how he lay down with 400 men who were machine-gunned systematically, up and down, and bombed by about 60 enemy aircraft; and in the end there was not a single casualty. Another chaplain was likewise machine-gunned and bombed as he lay on the beach, and when, after what seemed an eternity, he realized he had not been hit he rose to find that the sand all around where he had lain was pitted with bullet holes and that his figure was thus outlined on the ground.

'One thing can be certain about tomorrow's thanksgiving in our churches. From none will the thanks ascend with greater sincerity or deeper fervour than from the officers and men who have seen the Hand of God, powerful to save, delivering them from the hands of a mighty foe, who, humanly speaking, had them utterly at his mercy.'

Since the close of World War II fresh light has been thrown on the course of events by the publication of the official documents and records of the belligerents and the personal diaries and memoirs of statesmen, politicians and Service Chiefs. In consequence, many hitherto unexplained problems have been solved.

'Hitler Unnerved' and 'the Luftwaffe Grounded'

One such puzzle was why the Germans did not prevent the British Army reaching the coast at Dunkirk. In *The Struggle for Europe* (p. 19) Chester Wilmot states:

'Hitler was unnerved by his own success and was reluctant to drive on to the Channel until infantry had been brought up to cover the exposed flank. . . Although his fears had been unjustified, Hitler was now concerned lest the

French should succeed in forming a new front along the Somme. His eye was fixed on Paris, the ultimate political goal, not on Dunkirk, the immediate military objective.'

Furthermore, as Mr. Churchill reveals in his memoirs (*World War II,* vol. ii, p. 68) Hitler undoubtedly believed 'that his air superiority would be sufficient to prevent a large-scale evacuation by sea.' But the Fuehrer did not take the weather into his reckoning, for on May 30, General Halder, Chief of the German General Staff, complained in his diary: 'Bad weather has grounded the Luftwaffe and now we must stand by and watch countless thousands of the enemy getting away to England right under our noses.' Thus there is yet another testimony, this time from a German source, that the weather played a vital part in the deliverance at Dunkirk.

'We Serve an Unfolding Purpose'

With the fall of France the threat of a German invasion of the British Isles became a grave possibility. In a broadcast on July 14, Mr. Churchill said:

'Now it has come to us to stand alone in the breach and face the worst that the tyrant's might and enmity can do. Bearing ourselves humbly before God, but conscious that we serve an unfolding purpose, we are ready to defend our native land against the invasion by which it is threatened. We are fighting by ourselves alone; but we are not fighting for ourselves alone. Here in this strong City of Refuge which enshrines the title-deeds of human progress and is of deep consequence to Christian civilization; here, girt about by the seas and oceans where the Navy reigns; shielded from above by the prowess and devotion of our airmen—we await undismayed the impending assault. Perhaps it will come tonight. Perhaps it will come next week. Perhaps it will never come.'

Invasion never came, but was that a miracle? In the opinion of Mr. L. D. Gammans, M.P., it was, for in a memorable broadcast, 'War for the Soul of the British People,' he affirmed his faith thus:

'We often talk about the miracle of Dunkirk, but there was a far greater miracle which followed it, when the German Army, over two hundred divisions of them, flushed with victory, stood on the other side of the Channel, and all that we had here in trained, armed troops was less than one division. If that wasn't a miracle, what is a miracle? But why were we saved then? It was not that we could go back to our football matches, our dog tracks, our winter sports in Switzerland, our industrial squabbles and our party bickerings. I believe that we were saved then because, in spite of the past 20 years, there was still something worth saving, still a task that we had to do' (*The Listener,* 5.3.42).

Invasion—'Operation Sea Lion'

In his *World War II,* Mr. Churchill states: 'Soon after war broke out on September 3, 1939, the German Admiralty, as we have learned from their captured archives, began their Staff study of the invasion of Britain.' But in his well documented work, *Hitler's Strategy,* F. H. Hinsley, Lecturer in History in the University of Cambridge, draws attention to the fact that 'Hitler's own thorough plans for the attack on France contained no provision for a subsequent attempt to cross the Channel; nor did he regard the rapid success of the French operation as providing an opportunity for an invasion of England' (p. 64).

When Hitler looked across the Channel from Cap Gris Nez in the early days of June he saw only Britain's present plight—an army but no weapons—and he clung to the hope that Britain would capitulate. But he failed to allow for the British stubbornness which baulked Philip of Spain, Louis XIV, Napoleon and the Kaiser. As Chester Wilmot indicates, 'He did not appreciate the strength and courage her people drew instinctively from the past.'

Meanwhile, Admiral Raeder, Commander-in-Chief German Navy, had twice spoken to the Fuehrer about the plans for invasion but it was not until after due warning of Britain's true temper began to reach Berlin that on July

16 Hitler issued a directive regarding the invasion of England, which was given the code name of 'Sea Lion.'

On July 21 Hitler summoned his Chiefs of Staff and told them that he regarded the execution of operation 'Sea Lion' as 'the most effective method of bringing about a rapid conclusion of the war.' At the same time he warned them that invasion was 'an exceptionally bold and daring undertaking.' 'It is not just a river crossing,' he declared, 'but the crossing of a sea which is dominated by the enemy.' He stressed that 'complete mastery of the air' was the chief prerequisite and insisted that because of the possibility of unreliable weather 'the main operation must be completed by September 15.' This was a stiff demand and at ensuing Staff meetings there was vehement controversy between the Services. Nevertheless, as Mr. Churchill points out:

'These were great days for Nazi Germany. Hitler had danced his jig of joy before enforcing the humiliation of the French Armistice at Compiègne. The German Army marched triumphantly through the Arc de Triomphe and down the Champs Elysées. What was there they could not do? Why hesitate to play out a winning hand? Thus each of the three services involved in the operation "Sea Lion" worked upon the hopeful factors in their own theme and left the ugly side to their companions' (*World War II*, vol. ii, p. 272).

September 1940: The Weather 'Completely Abnormal'

However, the real responsibility for establishing the conditions in which invasion could be ventured was placed on the Luftwaffe which held the only key that could open the defences of the British Isles for the rest of the Wehrmacht.

Hitler gave operation 'Sea Lion' highest priority and ordered Admiral Raeder to intensify his efforts to mobilize the shipping resources of Western Europe. Every dockyard and slipway from Gdynia to Cherbourg was requisitioned for the construction and conversion of vessels which might be used in the operation. Mr. Churchill states:

'By the beginning of September the Naval Staff were able to report that the following had been requisitioned: 168 transports (of 700,000 tons), 1,910 barges, 419 tugs and trawlers, 1,600 motor-boats.

'All this Armada had to be manned, and brought to the assembly ports by sea and canal. Meanwhile since early July we had made a succession of attacks on the shipping in Wilhelmshaven, Kiel, Cuxhaven, Bremen, and Emden; and raids were made on small craft and barges in French ports and Belgian canals. When on September 1 the great southward flow of invasion shipping began it was watched, reported, and violently assailed by the Royal Air Force along the whole front from Antwerp to Havre' (ibid., p. 271).

But the fact that the Royal Air Force denied the enemy that degree of supremacy in the air, which was essential if the invasion was to be adequately prepared and launched, was not solely responsible for the postponement of the plan: unfavourable weather again greatly added to the German difficulties. Mr. Hinsley asserts:

'Great numbers of ships had to be moved to the embarkation area; and bad weather added to the difficulties. By September 6 the movement of barges was already behind schedule; minesweeping had not yet been possible on account of bad weather and interference by British aircraft. On September 10 it was still the case that the weather, "which for the time of the year is completely abnormal and unstable, greatly impairs transport movements and minesweeping" ' *(Hitler's Strategy,* p. 74).

It was at this stage becoming clear to the British Cabinet that if invasion was going to be undertaken it could not be long delayed. The increasing attacks by Bomber Command on the embarkation areas and the intensified bombardment by the Royal Navy on the invasion ports made it imperative for the enemy to keep their invasion vessels together; therefore on September 11 Mr. Churchill broadcast a stirring call to the nation in which he said:

'We must regard the next week or so as a very important period in our history. It ranks with the days when the Spanish Armada was approaching the Channel, and Drake was finishing his game of bowls; or when Nelson stood between us and Napoleon's Grand Army at Boulogne. We have read all about this in the history books; but what is happening now is on a far greater scale and of far more consequence to the life and future of the world and its civilization than these brave old days of the past.

'Every man and woman will therefore prepare himself to do his duty, whatever it may be, with special pride and care. . . . It is with devout but sure confidence that I say: Let God defend the Right.'

The Battle of Britain and the Demise of 'Sea Lion'

In the meantime, what Mr. Churchill describes as 'one of the decisive battles of the world' was being fought in the skies over the English Channel and the fields and towns of Southern England. In a mood of high confidence, Goering had told his commanders that by the exercise of air power Germany could counter the strategic advantages of Britain's island position. Once the R.A.F. had been annihilated, he said, the way would be clear for the launching of invasion—if Britain had not by then capitulated, which was still Hitler's fervent hope.

On July 10 the first phase of the long hard struggle began: attacks were launched on shipping in the Channel and on coastal towns whereby the Luftwaffe hoped to test, draw into battle and deplete the R.A.F., at the same time damaging towns marked as objectives for the forthcoming invasion. The second phase saw the attacks on airfields and R.A.F. installations, and the third, the attack on London.

In a speech on September 4 Hitler boasted that he would 'erase' our cities and the Nazi radio threatened, 'The German sword is about to strike with increasingly momentous strokes.' The great assault on London began on the afternoon of Saturday, September 7, when Goering sent over the largest force he could muster—more than one thousand bombers and fighters. Although the conflict in the air continued for several months, the crisis of the battle was in fact reached eight days later on September 15.

But, some time before, Sunday, September 8 had, by the desire of the King, been fixed as a Day of Prayer. At a service in Westminster Abbey, the final prayer began, 'Remember, O God, for good, these watchmen, who by day and by night climb into the air . . . Let Thy hand lead them, we beseech thee, and Thy right hand hold them.' How wonderfully God answered! A week later, on Sunday, September 15, Goering sent across the strongest escort ever provided, five fighters for every bomber, in the hope of saturating the defences—a venture which, to quote Chester Wilmot, 'set the seal on the Luftwaffe defeat.'

Goering had failed over London; Great Britain still fought back: a direct invasion would be necessary after all. But having failed to gain air supremacy, and with their fleet of invasion vessels severely battered, it was no longer possible for the Wehrmacht to launch it. Mr. Churchill writes:

'September 15 was the crux of the Battle of Britain. That same night our Bomber Command attacked in strength the shipping in the ports from Boulogne to Antwerp. At Antwerp particularly heavy losses were inflicted. On September 17, as we now know, the Fuehrer decided to postpone "Sea Lion" indefinitely. It was not till October 12 that the invasion was formally called off till the following spring. In July 1941 it was postponed again by Hitler till the spring of 1942, "by which time the Russian campaign will be completed." This was a vain but an important imagining. On February 13, 1942, Admiral Raeder had his final interview on "Sea Lion" and got Hitler to agree to a complete "stand-down." Thus perished operation "Sea Lion." And September 15 may stand as the date of its demise' (*World War II,* vol. ii, p. 297).

Divine Intervention Before & During the Battle of Britain

Speaking on an anniversary of this the greatest day of the battle of Britain, Air Chief Marshal Sir Hugh Dowding, who was Commander-in-Chief Fighter Command from its foundation in July 1936 and during the Luftwaffe onslaught, said that Britain was not too proud to recognize National Days of Prayer, and should therefore not be too proud to acknowledge the results of those prayers. His personal testimony regarding the Battle of Britain was given in an earlier speech quoted in the *Birmingham Daily Post* (8.6.42):

'I pay my homage to those gallant boys who gave their all that our nation might live. I pay my tribute to their leaders and commanders, but I say with absolute conviction that I can trace the intervention of God, not only in the battle itself, but in the events which led up to it; and that, if it had not been for this intervention, the battle would have been joined in conditions which, humanly speaking, would have rendered victory impossible.'

On yet another occasion Lord Dowding affirmed his belief in Divine Intervention, saying:

'Even during the Battle one realized from day to day how much external support was coming in. At the end of the Battle one had the feeling that there had been some special Divine Intervention to alter some sequence of events which would otherwise have occurred. I see that this intervention was no last minute happening. . . . It was all part of the mighty plan. It was the part that our dear country is to take in the regeneration of the world' (*Daily Sketch*, 15.9.43).

It must be stressed that these are the testimonies of one who, knowing all the facts, was in a position to speak with greater authority on the subject than any living man.

What form did the Divine Intervention 'in the events which led up to' the Battle of Britain take? It is not without good reason that Chester Wilmot directs attention to 'a series of inspired decisions dating back to 1934' which laid the foundation of the superior quality of British aircraft and technical equipment.

One of the decisions was that of the Air Staff to order 'a fighter with a maximum speed of more than 300 miles per hour and an armament of eight machine guns.' The outcome was the production of the Hurricane and the Spitfire possessing far greater hitting power than any foreign aircraft. The other major decision was to develop the discoveries of a Scottish scientist, Robert Watson-Watt, in connection with his use of radio waves for direction finding and range finding in order to follow the movement of thunderstorms—discoveries which were to provide the basis of a system giving long range warning of the approach of enemy aircraft and enabling their movements to be accurately plotted and therefore countered. 'At a demonstration in February, 1935,' writes Chester Wilmot, 'a primitive form of radar equipment picked up an aircraft at a range of eight miles. With a quickness of appreciation and a foresight seldom encountered when a service ministry is offered a revolutionary idea, the Air Council gave Watson-Watt the support he needed, and the Treasury provided the money for research.'

A Providential early warning
Letters to the Editor
The Daily Telegraph, January 3, 2006

SIR – The present Norwegian royal yacht helped to win the Battle of Britain. Sir Thomas Sopwith, for whom it was originally built, sent his chief engineer to Germany in 1936 to inspect the diesel engines that were to power his yacht, then under construction in Britain.

When the engineer also reported on the scale of German U-boat and aircraft manufacture, Sir Thomas immediately gave instruction for his firm to build hundreds of Hurricane fighters at his own expense, without an order from the Air Ministry. If these aircraft had not been ready in 1940, the outcome of war could have been very different.

Paul Weightman,
Dinsdale on Tees,
Co. Durham

The Weather and the Blitz
But, although Britain remained inviolate, it was not invulnerable. The German air assault continued on London, the industrial centres and the ports, doing immense damage. Mr. Churchill records:

'From September 7 to November 3 an average of two hundred German bombers attacked London every night. . . . The night raids were accompanied by more or less continuous daylight attacks by small groups or even single enemy planes, and the sirens often sounded at brief intervals throughout the whole twenty-four hours. To this curious existence the seven million inhabitants of London accustomed themselves. . . . Our outlook at this time was that London, except for its strong modern buildings, would be gradually and soon reduced to a rubble-heap' (*World War II,* vol. ii, pp. 302, 303, 309).

The climax of the mid-winter raids on London was on Sunday, December 29. Of this attack Mr. Churchill observes:

'All the painfully-gathered German experience was expressed on this occasion. It was an incendiary classic. The weight of the attack was concentrated upon the City of London itself. It was timed to meet the dead-low-water hour. The water-mains were broken at the outset by very heavy high-explosive parachute-mines. Nearly fifteen hundred fires had to be fought. . . . A void of ruin at the very centre of the British world gapes upon us to this day.' (ibid., p.333).

Yet, despite the great havoc caused, the German plans were to a very large degree frustrated. Under the heading, 'It's That Weather Again,' a *Daily Mail* (31.12.40) reporter wrote:

'Here are the real facts of Sunday night's fire-raising raid, as told to me yesterday: "It was one of the biggest night attacks on Britain since September. No R.A.F. night fighters were operating over the London area, though some were doing so between London and the coast. Soon after 10 p.m. the German Air Command sent out instructions for all the bombers then engaged to return to their bases, as the weather had taken a turn for the worse, and fog was blotting out their aerodromes." It was the weather, then, and not our night fighters that saved London from an even worse attack. The view is held that the assault was intended to be the fiercest of the war. Up to 1,000 bombers were to have been used during the night.'

Thus on still another occasion the elements were a vital factor. How many more such occurrences might be recorded!

The Chase and Sinking of the Bismarck

Towards the end of May 1941 a naval episode of highest consequences supervened in the Atlantic. On May 21 a German cruiser, *Prinze Eugen,* and the battleship *Bismarck,* the most powerful warship in the world, built regardless of treaty limitations and displacing 45,000 tons, left Bergen Fjord. In the early hours of the 24th, after being shadowed all night by the cruisers H.M.S. *Norfolk* and H.M.S. *Suffolk,* the enemy were engaged by H.M.S. *Hood* and H.M.S. *Prince of Wales.* Within a few minutes the *Hood* had been sunk and the *Prince of Wales* severely damaged. In his account of the incident Mr. Churchill writes:

'The *Bismarck* would indeed have been wise to rest content with what amounted by itself to a resounding triumph. She. . . . could go home to Germany with a major success. Her prestige and potential striking power would rise immensely, in circumstances difficult for us to measure or explain.

'Moreover, as we now know, she had been seriously injured by the *Prince of Wales,* and oil was leaking from her heavily. How then could she hope to discharge her mission of commerce destruction in the Atlantic? She had the choice of returning home victorious, with all the options of further enterprises open, or of going on to almost certain destruction. Only the extreme exaltation of her Admiral or the imperious orders by which he was bound can explain the desperate decision which he took' (*World War II,* vol. iii, p. 274).

The decision was to make for a French port: the two enemy battle cruisers *Scharnhorst* and *Gneisenau,* which during only two days in March had destroyed over 80,000 tons of shipping, together with the cruiser *Hipper,* were already at Brest.

The *Bismarck* was dogged by British cruisers and the *Prince of Wales*, but at 3 a.m. on the 25th radar contact was suddenly lost. At 10.30 a.m. a Coastal Command aircraft and two Swordfish from the *Ark Royal* spotted her once more. The Captain of H.M.S. *King George V*, in an article, 'The Chase and Sinking of the *Bismarck*,' in the *H.M. King George V Magazine*, describes the engagement from then onwards:

'The enemy was some 100 miles ahead of us and steaming at high speed, and it seemed only too probable that he would escape. Our hopes at this time were very low. There was still just time before dark for another torpedo bomber attack. A most successful attack in the face of heavy fire was delivered by the *Ark Royal*'s aircraft, and this resulted in several hits, one of which struck the *Bismarck*'s quarter and put her rudder out of action. This alone would not have stopped her flight. The *Bismarck,* however, could only steam into the wind. There was a fresh gale from the north-west, so she was forced to head straight for us. It is well here to remember the gale that scattered the Armada, the gale which brought Hawke's squadron tearing into Quiberon Bay and crashed the wrecks of Conflan's ships on to the rocks, and the calm of Dunkirk. There are many other examples in our naval history and they cannot be purely chance!'

Admiral Sir John Tovey, K.C.B., K.B.E., D.S.O., Commander-in-Chief, Home Fleet, also considered the sinking of the *Bismarck* a miracle. *Ashore and Afloat* (February, 1943) relates that, after the sinking, he spoke to the ship's company of H.M.S. *King George V* to this effect:

'One is very diffident about these things, but for a long time I have been a great believer in prayer. In the last few weeks I have prayed as I have never prayed before in my life. If anyone had said that we could meet the *Bismarck,* that great ship with her main armament of 9 in. and 15 in. guns unimpaired, and come out of the action without damage and without loss of a single British life, no one would have believed him. It is incredible. It can only be attributed to one thing. I firmly believe that the result of this action was due to Divine

Guidance and Intervention.'

Some years later, this same officer (now Lord Tovey), in a sermon broadcast from St. Dunstan's, Stepney, on January 30, 1949, again referred to the episode. Speaking of his life-long belief in prayer, he said:

'May I tell you of a particular experience of my own? It was during the pursuit of the *Bismarck.* One moment we seemed sure of getting her, and soon afterwards there didn't seem a hope. Finally, the *Bismarck* was hamstrung by a torpedo from an aircraft of the Fleet Air Arm from H.M.S. *Ark Royal,* and it only remained for me to go in in the morning with the *King George V* and the *Rodney* and finish her off. Although damaged below water the *Bismarck*'s gunnery was 100 per cent efficient, and if you had asked any experienced naval officer what would be the result of our engagement in the morning he would almost certainly have said: "You will sink her all right, but one or both of your ships will be seriously damaged." Just before I took the ships into action I went down to my fore-bridge cabin and went down on my knees to pray for guidance and help. I suddenly felt as if all responsibility had been taken off my shoulders and I knew everything would be all right. We engaged the *Bismarck* and sank her, and she did not score a single hit on any of our ships. To my mind there is only one possible explanation.'

The serious position which would have prevailed had the *Bismarck* escaped is now revealed by Mr. Churchill:

'Had she escaped the moral effects of her continuing existence as much as the material damage she might have inflicted on our shipping would have been calamitous. Many misgivings would have arisen regarding our capacity to control the oceans, and these would have been trumpeted round the world to our great detriment and discomfort' (*World War II,* vol. iii, p. 286).

Food in the Year of Greatest Need
It was not only in the battles on land, at sea and in the air that God's hand was to be seen. The people in beleaguered Britain must be fed, but the

shipping which should bring our food from overseas was urgently required for carrying men and munitions. The need was, therefore, for a bumper harvest in 1942. To this end a supreme effort was made by British agriculture and a degree of co-operation and united labour was achieved as never before in our history, added to which were the prayers of innumerable people that blessing might result. How those prayers were answered was revealed by Mr. R. S. Hudson, Minister of Agriculture, in a Postscript to the BBC 9 o'clock news on Old Michaelmas night 1942, when he said:

'But this also I would say to you, in humility and seriousness. Much hard work and technical skill have played their part in these mighty yields, amongst the richest of all time. But I believe that we have a higher Power to thank as well, and from the depths of our hearts.

'Some Power has wrought a miracle in the English harvest fields this summer, for in this, our year of greatest need, the land has given us bread in greater abundance than we have ever known before. The prayer, "Give us this day our daily bread," has in these times a very direct meaning for us all.'

That this Divine blessing continued is brought to notice in an article, 'This Wonderful Year,' by L. F. Easterbrook in the *News Chronicle* (6.5.43):

'Mr. Hudson was not ashamed to acknowledge last year the Divine Power that gave us a record harvest just when we most needed it. Can anyone doubt that the Power has been at work again? It has brought us through what might have been a very difficult winter with an unerring hand. For that we can be thankful for having sufficient fuel and sufficient milk, for wheat in the fields that never looked better, for grass in the meadows that has enabled winter feeding stuffs to be conserved, so that the small poultry keeper is now to get more food for his hens, and the housewife to get more milk for the family.

'We are still only half-way to harvest, and disasters can still happen. But nothing should take away our thankfulness for a season that has warmed and fed our bodies and cheered our hearts more generously than any dared hope.

If we have deserved it, we should feel proud, as well as humbly thankful.'

Malta and Sea Power

Mid-summer, 1942, was a time of sombre news from the Mediterranean and Middle East. By land and sea and air the scales seemed weighted against the British Forces. The series of events—sometimes strange events which were apparently chance accidents of history—leading to the complete change of fortune at El Alamein are worth reviewing in some detail.

The plight of Malta during this period of the war was serious in the extreme and that island base and fortress was of supreme importance: it not only enabled Britain to exercise Sea Power in the Mediterranean but it was also vital to our military strategy. An Admiralty writer describes its importance as follows:

'Malta was the fox gnawing into the vitals of Italy. It was Malta from which the British submarines slid out to take their toll of the Tripoli convoys; Malta that sent the Swordfish and Wellingtons to swoop on the tankers and ammunition ships whose cargoes were the very life of the dwindling Italian empire; Malta whose destroyers struck in the darkness and passed on unscathed, leaving death behind them. But if Malta were eliminated then there could be no stopping supplies to Rommel. Then there would be no stopping Rommel—Egypt, Suez, even perhaps India, to join hands there with Japan' (*The Mediterranean Fleet,* p. 73).

Similarly, Malta's position was affected in measure by the military situation in North Africa. In December 1941, the Eighth Army had occupied Benghazi, and shortly Egypt and Cyrenaica had been cleared of Axis forces except for those that reached El Agheila in retreat. Quite apart from more ambitious objectives, the position of Cyrenaica was extremely important because it gave us airfields from which cover could be given to convoys taking sorely needed supplies to Malta during the last and most hazardous part of their journey.

However, the benefit of these North African airfields to the beleaguered island did not long remain. Step by step the Eighth Army was forced back in a series of attacks and counter-attacks until on February 15, 1942, temporary equilibrium was reached near Gazala. During the lull, which lasted for over three months, the race became one to establish superiority of supplies and reinforcements. Describing the enemy's attempts to master the threat of Malta to Rommel's supplies, a War Office writer remarks:

'Geographically, his supply lines were short. He had only to get men and supplies across the Mediterranean to Benghazi or Tripoli, to be able to wheel them up to the front. His main task, therefore, was to neutralize Malta as a focus of interruption. That is why, all through the spring, huge Axis forces based on Sicily pounded the island without respite. The defence was beyond praise, but there could be no effective offensive either by sea or air' (*The Eighth Army*, p. 35).

The fact that in spite of its vulnerability Malta did remain inviolate can only be ascribed to the over-ruling of a covenant-keeping God. The distinguished historian, Arthur Bryant, observed in a broadcast: '"Wherever there is water to float a ship," said Napoleon, "or man could sail, I was sure to find you in the way." And Hitler found us in the way too. Gibraltar, Malta and Alexandria—the triple pillars of our Mediterranean strategy held.' Mr. Bryant had much else to say of British Sea Power, as will many an historian in the future. This possession of Sea Power, dependent as it is on the necessary world-wide bases, is no chance blessing. It is the consequence of a promise made long ago to Abraham upon the oath of Jehovah: 'By Myself have I sworn, saith the Lord . . . thy seed shall possess the gate of his enemies' (*Genesis* 22:16-17).

The Epic of Malta

'Wars and battles are not won by material means, important as these are,' declared General Sir William Dobbie, G.C.M.G., K.C.B., D.S.O., and Governor of Malta during the height of the Island's ordeal, in a broadcast entitled, 'The Epic Story of Malta.' In the end,' he added, 'it is, under God, the men and the spirit which count. . . I am convinced that God for Christ's sake still does answer prayer. . . . . The acknowledgment of God, through Christ, and trust in Him, is now as ever that which matters most.' This great Christian soldier describes his experiences at Malta in detail in his book, *A Very Present Help*:

'It was obvious to us that our human resources were woefully inadequate, and many of us were constrained to turn our eyes to "the hills, from whence cometh my help." God's Word was a great standby to me, and doubtless to many others, too, at this time. In it I read how God had helped His people in old times when they were faced with situations similar to that confronting us. And God reminded us that although outward circumstances have changed since those days in many ways, and although the problem might be enunciated in different words, yet God, the solver of problems, does not change. He is the same today as He has ever been, and "His hand is not shortened that it cannot save." The difficulty is likely to rest with us, either that we do not exercise the simple faith which lays hold on that power, or that our "iniquities separate between us and God," so that He cannot use it on our behalf. Many persons in Malta, both in responsible and other positions, did, I think, realize our need of His help, and were prepared to ask Him to give it us. By no other means could we be sure of holding this vital outpost of Empire, and so we turned to Him Who alone is the giver of victory. . . .

'I humbly believe that God, in His mercy, answered the prayers offered to Him in this way, and in the two years and more of the siege which followed His help was very obvious and very real.

'The Lord Your God Shall Fight for You'

'At about the same time, I was greatly encouraged by a telegram I received from the Chief of the Imperial General Staff, General Sir Edmund Ironside (later, Field-Marshal Lord Ironside). It showed me that others in high places at home were thinking along the same lines as we were in Malta. The telegram, which was addressed to me personally, contained the reference, "*Deuteronomy*, chapter 3, verse 22." I looked up the reference in my Bible, and I read: "Ye shall not fear them: for the Lord your God He shall fight for you." This was a very welcome and timely reminder of a great and well-proved truth, and, coming as it did from a person in his position, and being addressed to one in mine, in view of the special circumstances of the time, it meant much to us.

'I have said that the help which God gave was very obvious and real. The same help was noticed at the time of the withdrawal from Dunkirk, and during the "Battle of Britain." It certainly was so in the "Battle of Malta." During the two years which followed the declaration of war by Italy, God's protecting hand was so much in evidence that people were noticing it, and remarking on it. On a number of occasions officers have come to me and said quite spontaneously: "Do you know, sir, I think that Someone up there (pointing upwards) has been helping us today." I no doubt replied, "Yes, I think so too," and I may have added, "You may remember we asked Him to help us, and today we have been watching Him doing it." Such a conversation took place not once nor twice, but a number of times.

'God's restraining hand continued to be strong for us for a long period. It was not just one instantaneous act of deliverance, it was a long drawn out process.

'We have found how prone we are to limit the help that God gives. We say, "He has undoubtedly helped us so far—but we cannot expect Him to go on doing so indefinitely." We seem to imagine that God's help is subject to the law of averages or of mathematical probabilities. Thank God, that is not so. Such a thought is dishonouring to our Heavenly Father. He can deliver us not only for a day, but for a week, a month, a year, or for any other period. He can go on delivering us for as long as He sees we need deliverance. That is one of the lessons He graciously taught us in the Siege of Malta.

'But although we did not experience the invasion we expected, yet we were immediately subjected to another form of attack, aerial bombardment. I have already shown how ill-prepared we were to meet it. Not only had we hardly any fighter aircraft, and a very meagre number of anti-aircraft guns, but the dense population of Malta rendered this form of attack peculiarly dangerous. In the early morning of June 11, 1940, the Italian bombers came over Malta and dropped their loads, causing much devastation and many casualties, especially among the civil population. This attack was repeated many times that day, and on many subsequent days, until these visitations became the commonplace experiences of the everyday life of the people of Malta. By the time we left Malta, some two years later, the fortress had been subjected to over 2,000 bombing attacks.

'These first attacks were delivered at a time when the British Empire had had very little actual experience of air attack. . . . But in spite of all these and unknown perils, the people of Malta stood up to the ordeal in a truly remarkable way, and adapted themselves to the trying circumstances with commendable aptitude and resolute determination. Was it their innate realization of God, and their trust in Him, that brought them through their hard trials with flying colours? I think it was, and I think they would say that it was' (pp. 82-86).

At the Gates of Cairo

So Malta stood under God's protection. The lull in Cyrenaica was eventually broken on May 27. But the fighting went badly for the Eighth Army, and, after a little more than two weeks of desperate and confused armoured battles, Gazala was evacuated on the night of June 13-14.

Catastrophe followed quickly at Tobruk. This fortress, which had earlier withstood eight months of siege, was overrun on June 21, and 25,000 men of the garrison fell into Rommel's hands.

The seriousness of the situation was frankly admitted by Mr. Churchill in the House of Commons. In the course of a debate on July 2, he said:

'The military misfortunes of the last fortnight in Cyrenaica and Egypt have completely transformed the situation, not only in that theatre, but throughout the Mediterranean. We have lost upwards of 50,000 men, by far the larger proportion of whom are prisoners, a great mass of material, and in spite of carefully organized demolitions, large quantities of stores have fallen into the enemy's hands. Rommel has advanced nearly 400 miles through the desert, and is now approaching the fertile Delta of the Nile. . . . We are at this moment in the presence of a recession of our hopes and prospects in the Middle East and in the Mediterranean unequalled since the fall of France.'

On came Rommel and the Africa Korps, headlong for Suez. Sollum, Sidi Barrani and Mersa Matruh, each in turn were occupied by the enemy. German bombers were over the fleet's base at Alexandria. General Auchinleck, the Commander-in-Chief Middle East, decided to make a last-ditch stand at El Alamein. Here, during the summer, he had the skeleton of prepared positions constructed, and now he reaped the reward of foresight.

The retreating and frustrated Eighth Army reached the Alamein line of defence on Monday, June 29. On the Wednesday, the German wireless boasted in English that General Rommel and the Afrika Korps would be sleeping in Alexandria on Saturday night. It certainly seemed that Rommel would keep this appointment, for on the night before the promised date the German armour, having breached the Alamein Line, went into leaguer a bare 40 miles from the city. A moment had come when all Islam and Christendom held its breath.

A Drink that Made History

The description of events on the following days must be left to the pen of Major Peter W. Rainier, who had been appointed by the British General Staff to supervise the construction of a pipeline from the Nile Delta out into the desert so that water for their forces might be pumped to the battle line. In his book, *Pipeline to Battle,* he remarks:

'July 4 was the critical day. To counter the German thrust Auchinleck had massed the battle-scarred remnant of his tank forces, together with what he had been able to collect from repair shops back at base. The two armoured forces met, supported by infantry. . . . Both sides were deadly tired. There was nothing brilliant about the fight. The side that could longest sustain an uninspired pounding would win.

'The Afrika Korps gave first. After a couple of hours of fumbling, Rommel's forces began to withdraw. The high tide of invasion had been stemmed. Never again would the invaders reach so near their goal of the Egyptian Delta. The Panzer divisions with their enlorried infantry rolled sullenly back westward, but our men were too weary to drive their advantage home.

'Then, as the battle broke off, an astonishing thing happened. More than 1,100 Germans walked across to our line with their hands in the air. Thirst had done it. Their tongues were literally hanging out of their mouths. For thirty-six hours they had had no fresh water to drink. That pipeline, full of salt water, was the cause. They had found and gleefully tapped it. The sea water in it had increased their thirst almost to the point of delirium' (p. 127).

'For 1,100 of them to surrender when escape lay open—that was nothing short of a miracle!' comments Major Rainier in an article in *Reader's Digest* entitled: 'A Drink that made History.' He continues:

'Why was that pipeline full of salt water? As the officer responsible for supplying the Eighth Army with water through all its desert campaigns, I can give you the answer. The pipeline was a new one, and I never wasted precious fresh water in testing a line; I always used salt water. If the Panzers had punched through Alamein the day before, that pipeline would have been empty. Two days later it would have been full of fresh water. As it happened, the Nazis got salt water, and they didn't detect the salt at once because their sense of taste had already been anaesthetized by the brackish water they had been used to and by thirst.

'The balance of the crucial desert battle was so even that I believe the enemy—without that salted torture—might have outlasted us. And then defenceless Alexandria would have fallen into their hands. On so small a turn of fate is history written!'

The enemy accepted this check, and on the very next day began to set up an anti-tank screen. But the chagrin of the Axis was considerable. Mussolini had hurried to Africa in order to head victory parades into Alexandria and Cairo, and there was some difficulty in explaining that he had only come to inspect troops. The German brass bands specially imported had to be silenced and hidden!

The Hinge of Fate

All through August both sides were hard at work regrouping, extending their minefields, probing for information and collecting reinforcements. Early in August the Prime Minister paid a visit to the Eighth Army. The first result of his visit was the reorganization of the Command and the Army. General Alexander, who had been the last man to leave Dunkirk and had subsequently brought our small forces practically intact out of Burma, was appointed Commander-in-Chief.

General 'Strafer' Gott, the famous and trusted leader of the XIIIth Corps, was designated to command the Eighth Army, but he was killed when an enemy fighter intercepted the plane in which he was travelling to Cairo. As second choice, the command was entrusted to General Montgomery, who, while holding an appointment in England, had achieved a great reputation for force of character and for insistence upon physical fitness in every officer and man under his command. Within 48 hours of General Montgomery's arrival, every man in Egypt knew that a fresh wind was blowing and that their new Commander was something quite different, something unique. However, it was not only the character and physical fitness of his men that General Montgomery wished to build up. There was something deeper. As he has since declared: 'The soldiers must have faith in God and not think lightly of the moral things involved.' To achieve his objective, General Montgomery enlisted the aid of his padres. To quote his own words: 'When overseas I called on my chaplains to help me in my task, and right well did they answer the call.' It was not long before the new spiritual tone of the Eighth Army became talked about in England.

On September 3, the anniversary of the outbreak of war, a National Day of Prayer was held—for the first time on a weekday. In the opinion of many it was observed far more sincerely and universally than any of its predecessors.

General Montgomery laid his plans carefully and, before the battle was joined, he issued his inspiring order to the Eighth Army: 'Let us pray that the Lord, mighty in battle, will give us the victory.' And what a victory it was! At 9.40 precisely on the night of October 23 our guns opened up. The historic battle of El Alamein had begun. According to Mr. Churchill: 'It marked, in fact, the turning of "the hinge of fate." It may also be said, "Before Alamein we never had a victory. After Alamein we never had a defeat" ' (*World War II*, vol. iv, p.541).

The Eighth Army swept on with scarcely a pause, and by November 11 the Axis had been driven out of Egypt. Meanwhile, the pattern of allied victory was being revealed. The Eighth Army now formed the eastern arm of pincers which were to squeeze the enemy out of North Africa. The western arm of the pincers was provided by the new front in North-West Africa.

'More Than Planning Here'

On November 8 the British and American armies landed at Algiers and Oran in Algeria and at Casablanca in French Morocco. The good hand of God was also to be seen in the opening stages of this operation.

In his memoirs, *A Sailor's Odyssey*, Admiral Sir Andrew Cunningham, who was Naval Commander-in-Chief for the operation, reveals that the date of the assault was governed by the necessity to land the American troops on the open Moroccan beaches near Casablanca before the weather deteriorated, although various circumstances eventually forced its postponement until as late as the beginning of the second week in November.

Describing this, the first great amphibious operation of the war, Mr. Churchill reveals:

'The first of the "Torch" convoys left the Clyde on October 22. By the 26th all the fast troopships were under way and American forces were sailing for Casablanca direct from the United States. The whole of the expedition of about 650 ships was now launched upon the enterprise. They traversed the Bay of Biscay or the Atlantic unseen by the U-boats or by the Luftwaffe.

'All our resources were at full strain. Far to the north our cruisers watched the Denmark Strait and the exits from the North Sea to guard against intervention by enemy surface ships. Others covered the American approach near the Azores, and Anglo-American bombers attacked the U-boat bases along the French Atlantic seaboard. Despite apparent U-boat concentrations towards the Gibraltar Straits, the leading ships began to enter the Mediterranean on the night of November 5-6 still undetected. It was not until the 7th, when the Algiers convoy was less than twenty-four hours from its destination, that it was sighted, and even then only one ship was attacked' (*World War II*, vol. iv, p. 545).

Admiral Cunningham states:

'The defence for the "Torch" convoys was marshalled in strength. But no imaginable defence could altogether have warded off the concentrated attacks of thirty to forty U-boats. The procession of large convoys converging on the Straits of Gibraltar passed close enough to submarine concentrations, but it is the almost incredible fact that they were not attacked and sustained no casualties' (*A Sailor's Odyssey,* p. 482).

'How Great a Part Providence Has Played'

After pointing out the supreme importance of the capture of Casablanca, the French naval base and Headquarters of the naval and military forces in Morocco, Admiral Cunningham continues:

'As I have said, the landing beaches were open to the Atlantic and success depended largely on the weather. On November 6, when Admiral Hewitt was nearing his destination, the forecasts from Washington and London for D-Day were anything but encouraging: "Surf 15 feet high and landings impossible." The meteorologist with Admiral Hewitt, however, considered the storm was moving too rapidly to have any adverse effect on the beaches, and predicted that the weather would moderate and make landing possible.

'Admiral Hewitt had to make a most difficult decision. If he ignored the forecasts from Washington and London and decided to stick to the Casablanca plan he must deploy his forces on November 7, the eve of D-day. If he attempted the landings in adverse weather the results might be disastrous. If, on the other hand, he adopted the alternative plan of entering the Mediterranean, he might meet a heavy concentration of enemy submarines, and in any case would have to land the troops on the largely unsurveyed beaches between Oran and the frontier of Spanish Morocco. Moreover, if he elected to land there it would have left untouched at the outset a considerable part of the French Army and Navy in North Africa.

'The Admiral chose the bolder course, and at midnight on November 6-7 decided to risk the weather and go for Casablanca. Fortune favoured him. The sea went down, and on November 7, his large collection of ships was approaching the coast in fair weather with a north-easterly wind and a smooth sea' (ibid., p. 491).

The assault phase not only at Casablanca but at Algiers and other objectives in the Mediterranean was, according to Mr. Churchill, 'a brilliant success.' Under the heading, 'Make it a Call to Prayer,' G. Ward Price wrote in the *Daily Mail* (14.11.42):

'Only the thoughtless can fail to realize how great a part Providence has played in the swift and successful transformation of the war—a situation upon which our hopes are henceforth founded. Those who have heard something of the inside story of the dramatic events of this historic week are reminded of that Dispensation that smoothed the waters at Dunkirk.

'The Allied General Staff had been warned by weather experts that after October 1 the Atlantic swell off the coast of Morocco would probably be too high for landing operations. So it was—with the exception of last Sunday— the date for which the landing had been planned.

'In this sceptics may see no more than a fortunate coincidence; but it is not the only feature of a great undertaking that will suggest to others the need for expressing their gratitude to God when the victory bells begin their cheering chimes.'

Christian Commanders

The Commander-in-Chief of the Anglo-U.S. forces engaged in these landings and in the subsequent campaign in Tunisia was General Eisenhower, with General Anderson in command of the British First Army. Like so many victorious leaders in the history of both the British and American peoples, these Generals were Christian men of high ideals. Typical of General Anderson was the conclusion of a Foreword in a book issued to all ranks describing French North Africa, which read as follows: 'Our fathers of old were never ashamed to ask God's blessing on their enterprises. Let us therefore unashamedly and humbly ask God's help in our endeavours and strive to deserve it.'

The Axis forces stubbornly resisted the Allied armies under General Eisenhower's command and also General Montgomery's Eighth Army. Relentlessly the pincers closed around the enemy in Tunisia and by May 12, 1943, all organized resistance had ceased. The campaign in Tunisia had cost the Axis 340,000 men and great quantities of material. The official publication, *Tunisia,* concludes with these words: 'Military historians will probably rank the victory as the most perfect example of a battle achieving that at which all commanders aim, the ending of a war by the total elimination of the enemy . . . Tunis, the last battle of the war in Africa, will stand as the classic example of complete achievement.' As Mr. Churchill averred in a speech to the United States Congress on May 19: 'For us, arrived at this milestone in the war: we can say "One Continent redeemed".'

This victorious campaign along the North African seaboard culminating in the rout of the Axis armies followed closely what the *Daily Sketch* (7.5.43) describes as 'an impressive renaissance in spiritual values. . . in all ranks of the fighting services.' The truth of this statement is confirmed from many sources. The Bishop of Rochester in his *Diocesan Chronicle* said: 'The most religious body of Englishmen today is the Eighth Army. We are also told how many outstanding Christians there are among the paratroops.' Moreover, General Anderson, when discussing the arrangements for the Thanksgiving Service in which all ranks of the First Army took part, declared: 'Sometimes we are too apt to take credit to ourselves for our accomplishments and not to thank the Almighty enough for His part. There is a great spiritual force as well as physical forces at work in our Army in this War' (*The Daily Telegraph*, 14.5.43).

'Preserved for Some Purpose'

It was at about this time that Sir Archibald Sinclair (now Viscount Thurso), Air Minister, gave his testimony to over-ruling by the Almighty when addressing the General Assembly of the Church of Scotland:

'We have been most miraculously preserved. We must have been preserved for some purpose, and we must seek humbly to discover what that purpose is and be faithful to it.

'When I think of the wonderful change that has come over the fortunes of war, I feel that we must indeed be grateful. The bows of the mighty men are broken and they that stumbled are now girded with strength.

'I feel sure that we must strive to the utmost for victory, and when we get victory it will solve none of the great problems which are troubling our hearts and minds, but it will give us opportunity.

'Then the question will come: what use we. . . shall make of that opportunity. The thing that seems clear to me is that we shall not succeed in making the most of that opportunity if we forsake the commandments of God' (*Evening Standard*, 21.5.43).

Neither, as will be seen later, was Sir Archibald Sinclair alone in his belief that we 'have been preserved for a purpose.'

The Invasion of Sicily

A new stage of the war began with the invasion of Sicily on July 10, 1943. The amphibious phase of this campaign brought further confirmation that God answers the prayers of those who call upon Him in faith. The full story of this great barrage of prayer that was offered up for blessing upon this operation may never be told, although at the time many revealing incidents were reported in the Press and on the radio. For example, Ross Monro, Press correspondent with the Canadian Forces, describes an incident which occurred on the H.Q. ship the day before the attack:

'The officers met in the lounge. "We are on the eve of a never-to-be-forgotten night in the history of the world," said the colonel. "We will remember this night and our children will." Everyone repeated the Lord's Prayer, shook hands all round, and the meeting broke up' (*The Daily Telegraph,* 12.7.43).

Again, a special correspondent on board a destroyer related how the Captain mustered all hands on deck to explain the part the ship would play in the invasion, concluding his remarks with the words: 'I have every faith in God, and in you,' after which he read the prayer Nelson uttered on the eve of Trafalgar:

'May the Great God Whom I worship grant to my country and for the benefit of Europe in general a great and glorious victory, and may no misconduct in anyone tarnish it.

'May humanity after victory be the predominant feature in the British Fleet. For myself, individually, I commit my life to Him Who made me, and may His blessing alight on my endeavours for serving my country faithfully; to Him I resign myself and the just cause which is entrusted to me to defend.'

Eisenhower: '. . . .Events Are in the Hands of God'

Yet another incident on this historic eve of the invasion of Sicily is related by the Rev. W. H. Elliott in an article entitled, 'The Faith of a General,' in the *Sunday Graphic* (28.5.44):

'The man was standing, silhouetted sharp and clear in the moonlight, on the crest of a little hill, looking out to sea. In front of him glittered a wide expanse of waters. Near him on that hill top was a group of other men, watching what he watched, and without a word.

'They were watching a great company of ships, a most wonderful sight indeed, big ships and little ships, hundreds of them, thousands of them, grey monsters on the sky line, quick darting destroyers, troop-ships, tankers, freighters, almost down to tugs and boats—all full of men.

'A great moment, tense, historic, a moment of silence, too, were it not for all the planes, hundreds of them, buzzing, zooming, circling overhead and over those ships. But a man can be silent anywhere— within himself.

'Suddenly, said an eye-witness, the man drew himself stiffly to attention. He lifted his hand to the salute, and so for some minutes he remained. Then he dropped his hand and bent his head, once again motionless, quiet. He was praying. Well he might, with that great Armada setting out for Sicily and he commanding them. Thank Heaven he was, and is, one of that sort.

'Presently he turned to the group beside him—to one of his aides. "There comes a time," he said, "when you have done all that you can possibly do; when you have used your brains, your training, your technical skill, and the die is cast, and events are in the hands of God —and there you have to put them."

'So General Eisenhower, for he was the man. You may have heard the story before, but it is well worth pondering again. That was how he felt about the Sicily invasion. That was how he carried the crushing weight of his responsibility. How would you like to carry such a responsibility? But he at least knows the Power that can uphold him. He, as did Abraham Lincoln in like case, knows where to go.'

The Armada Medal. (page 7)

The National Day of Prayer, May 26, 1940. The scene at Westminster Abbey.
(page 13)

The Withdrawal from Dunkirk. (page 14)

So Near and Yet So Far - the invasion which never took place. A photograph which appeared in German newspapers in 1940 showing Goering and his staff gazing across the Channel at the white cliffs of Dover. (page 18)

Christ Church, Portsdown. The Knights' Vigil, June 4, 1944. (page 56)

Photo by Bob Danvers-Walker

'On June 4th, 1944, forty-eight hours before the invasion of Normandy, Head-quarters Second Army held a service of dedication for battle in this church. To commemorate that service and the great events which followed these two windows were dedicated on June 6th, 1948.' (page 56)

Men of the Army of Liberation taking part in an Eve of the Battle Service aboard a landing craft. The service is being conducted by a chaplain of the United States Army. (page 55)

The Sign in the Heavens as the Invasion Forces went in. The great rainbow which spread over the whole area at dawn on June 6 as the troops went in to land on the beaches at the beginning of the liberation of Europe. A special drawing for THE SPHERE, *by Roland Davies.* (page 64)

A B-29 bomber (page 71)

Part of the Task Force leaving Portsmouth in April 1982. (page76)

Pilots scrambling to their planes. Battle of Britain, 1940. (page 21)

The siege of Malta, 1942. (page 30)

The Motor Church of St. George, driven by a padre, follows the Eighth Army. Many countries of the Commonwealth were represented in the materials used for the Church, which was built upon a W.D. type A.E.C. Chassis. (page 37)

Men of the First Army gathered in the ruins of the vast amphitheatre at Carthage, where in the early days of Christianity thousands of martyrs perished for their faith. On this occasion the ceremony was one of thanksgiving for the victories in North Africa. General Anderson, C.-in-C. of the First Army, read the lesson. Our picture shows senior officers leaving after the service. (page 52)

The fact that God did answer these and countless other prayers which were offered up is evident from the broadcast, 'The Greatest Armada in History,' by Commander Anthony Kimmins:

'As we rendezvoused at sea, our own force looked almost big enough to do the job by itself: escorting warships, big troopships with their assault-craft hanging on the davits, and literally hundreds of other landing-craft steaming under their own power. And yet we knew we were only a tiny part of the whole.

'Beyond the horizon there were other forces, some even larger than our own, approaching Sicily to arrive with us dead on zero hour. But although we could not see them, we knew that there was one thing which was worrying them just as much as us—the weather. By all the rules one expects fine weather and a calm sea in the Mediterranean at this time of the year, but now it suddenly started to blow, a real blow, Force 6, half a gale, from the north-west. This meant that it would be blowing down the coast and that many of the beaches would have little lee. The surf would be terrific, and it would be almost impossible for our landing-craft to force their way through and land their precious cargoes intact. We hoped and prayed that with sunset the wind would drop, but as the sun dipped over the horizon the wind if anything seemed to grow stronger. It was a strange and, to me anyhow, a terrifying feeling. In spite of everything that man's ingenuity could do to produce the most modern and up-to-date ships and landing-craft; in spite of all the elaborate preparations: here we were, in the long run, at the mercy of the elements. The memory of how a gale had sealed the fate of the Spanish Armada sent a nasty chill down one's spine. Foul weather: the eternal enemy of the sailor. But there was nothing to be done about it, and the ships ploughed on with many of the smaller craft taking it over green as they wallowed in the high seas.

'But there was no turning back now, and as the darkness closed down and the ships ploughed on, I couldn't help thinking of some of the miracles of weather which had already favoured us in this war: Dunkirk; North Africa.

Perhaps three times was too much to expect. Perhaps . . . and then it happened. With barely an hour and a half to go before zero hour the wind suddenly dropped, the white horses disappeared, and the swell went down quicker than I have ever seen it do before. It was so sudden it was almost unbelievable, and as people stared into the darkness it seemed miraculous, as if. . . . well, put it this way, many a silent prayer of thanks was offered up' (*The Listener*, 22.7.43).

That the earlier unfavourable weather was actually a blessing in disguise has since been revealed by Admiral Cunningham who was in command of the Allied Naval Forces:

'At many places along the Sicilian coast the enemy garrisons had been on the alert for weeks. One expected that the Italians might even maintain offshore patrols. But the garrisons, lulled into a sense of security by the wild weather, and believing that no one would attempt a landing in such conditions, allowed their vigilance to relax. Syracuse and Augusta were quite close; but the Italian sailors apparently confined their small craft to harbour and themselves to bed' (*A Sailor's Odyssey*, p. 551).

The successful campaign in Sicily was soon followed by the invasion of the mainland of Italy and Mussolini's dramatic downfall; it marked, as President Roosevelt declared, 'the beginning of the end.'

The Task of God's Servants

At the close of 1943 the invasion of France was the major task for the year ahead, but in Britain and America confidence was tempered by the knowledge that heavy sacrifices might be involved. For example an editorial in *The Daily Telegraph* (12.12.43) remarked:

'Both the British and American forces may have to endure the greatest sacrifice of life which they have yet suffered. We in this country may again come under heavy air attack. But the courage and fortitude which brought the Allies through their greatest perils and well on the road to victory cannot falter now as we go forward to bring back peace and good will, "to bind up the broken-hearted, to proclaim liberty to the captives, and the opening of the prison to them that are bound".'

The writer of the article was justified in quoting *Isaiah* 61:1, for despite the fact that this verse in its primary setting refers to Christ, it also proclaims the mission of His servant nations. The prophet further reveals the task that God would have His servants undertake, namely, 'to loose the bands of wickedness, to undo the heavy burdens, and to let the oppressed go free . . . to deal thy bread to the hungry, and . . . when thou seest the naked, that thou cover him' (*Isaiah* 58:6, 7).

Simultaneously with the building up of the British and American forces for the liberation of Europe, the United Nations Relief and Rehabilitation Administration was preparing plans for the succour of the distressed peoples when they were freed.

That the relief subsequently rendered by this organization would have been non-existent but for British and United States support is revealed in *The History of UNRRA* (vol. iii, p. 500) where the contributions received from member Governments for the period of operations are tabulated. The amounts contributed by the United States, Britain and the other nations of the British Commonwealth account for no less than 95 per cent of the grand total!

At that time it was pointed out in *The National Message* (19.1.44) that when considering the hazards of crossing the Channel and storming the Nazi citadel, comfort and assurance would be found in many of the messages of the prophets to God's people as for example, 'But now, the Eternal promises, He Who created you, O Jacob, He Who made you, O Israel, "Fear not, for I redeem you, I claim you, you are Mine. I will be with you when you pass through the waters, no rivers shall overflow you; when you pass through fire, you shall not be scorched, no flames shall burn you" ' (*Isaiah* 43:1, Moffatt).

Return and 'He Will Deliver You'

How great and mighty were the deliverances which God wrought on behalf of His people Israel in days of old! In spite of their sin and waywardness, again and again miracles were performed to save them when they repented and turned to God for help.

Memorable indeed was Israel's deliverance from bondage in Egypt. The plagues upon Egypt and the Egyptians (*Exodus* 7-12), the crossing of the Red Sea by Israel and the engulfing of the hosts of Pharaoh (*Exodus* 14) were events never to be forgotten in Israel's history, special instructions being given to ensure their remembrance from generation to generation.

The fall of the fortress of Jericho was another example of God's intervention for His people. Archaeological excavations conducted by Professor Garstang on the site of the city confirm that the walls fell down and the city was burnt as described in *Joshua 6.*

On many occasions in the period of the Judges it is recorded that 'the children of Israel cried unto the Lord' and He delivered them from their enemies (*Judges* 2:18; 3:9, 15; 4:3, 23; 10:10, 15, 16; 11:32), the most notable occasion being when Gideon's contemptible little army of 300 put to flight the mighty hosts of 'all the Midianites and the Amalekites and the children of the east' (*Judges* 6-7).

In the days of Samuel a religious revival and a great deliverance followed the exhortation of the prophet: 'If ye do return unto the Lord with all your hearts . . . and prepare your hearts unto the Lord, and serve Him only . . . He will deliver you out of the hand of the Philistines' (I *Samuel* 7:3). Israel turned to God and 'the Lord thundered with a great thunder on that day upon the Philistines, and discomfited them; and they were smitten before Israel' (I *Samuel* 7:10).

In the history of Judah many revivals occurred, often at the instigation of the king, and these were always followed either by victory, if war was in progress, or by continued peace. For example, 'Asa did that which was good and right in the eyes of the Lord his God . . . and commanded Judah to seek the Lord God of their fathers, and to do the law and the commandment. Also he took away out of all the cities of Judah the high places and the images; and the kingdom was quiet before him' (II *Chronicles* 14:2, 4, 5).

When Judah were threatened by Ammon and Moab, Jehoshophat led a great revival calling to remembrance the promises made by God to Solomon after the latter's prayer at the dedication of the temple (I *Kings* 8:23-53; II *Chronicles* 7:12-22). The reply came: 'Thus saith the Lord unto you, Be not afraid nor dismayed by reason of this great multitude; for the battle is not yours but God's. Ye shall not need to fight in this battle: set yourselves, stand ye still, and see the salvation of the Lord with you' (II *Chronicles* 20:15, 17). The next morning it was discovered that the enemy had destroyed themselves in mutual combat. 'And the fear of God was on all the kingdoms of those countries, when they had heard that the Lord fought against the enemies of Israel. So the realm of Jehoshaphat was quiet: for his God gave him rest round about' (II *Chronicles* 20:29-30).

King Hezekiah, from the very first year of his reign, sought to do the will of God, and the religious revival for which he was so largely responsible was followed by a most spectacular deliverance (II *Chronicles* 29-32; II *Kings* 18, 19). Sennacherib, King of Assyria, invaded Judah, and before besieging Jerusalem, sought to terrify the defenders of the city by propaganda. There is a striking parallel between the mixture of threats and specious promises used by present-day totalitarian propagandists and the methods of the ancient Assyrians when seeking to undermine the morale of their opponents (II *Kings* 18:28-32). In a message to Hezekiah, Sennacherib adopted a defiant and blasphemous attitude to God, saying:

'Let not thy God in whom thou trustest deceive thee, saying, Jerusalem shall not be delivered into the hand of the king of Assyria. Behold, thou hast heard what the kings of Assyria have done to all lands, by destroying them utterly: and shalt thou be delivered?'

The narrative continues:

'And Hezekiah received the letter. . . . and read it: and Hezekiah went up into the house of the Lord, and spread it before the Lord. And Hezekiah prayed before the Lord, and said . . . Now therefore, O Lord our God, I beseech thee, save Thou us out of his hand, that all the kingdoms of the earth may know that Thou art the Lord God, even Thou only. . . . And it came to pass that night, that the angel of the Lord went out, and smote in the camp of the Assyrians an hundred four-score and five thousand: and when they arose early in the morning, behold, they were all dead corpses. So Sennacherib king of Assyria departed, and went and returned, and dwelt at Nineveh' (II *Kings* 19:10-36).

Montgomery: 'Let God Arise . . . .'

On March 24, a great speech was made at the Mansion House by General Montgomery—a speech which ranks with the many memorable utterances by leaders of the Israel people as they made ready for battle.

General Montgomery, pleading for the help of the whole nation in the task of inspiring our soldiers, averred:

'Only from an inspired nation can go forth, under these conditions, an inspired army. When our men go forth to battle on this great endeavour—that is the time when there must swell up in the nation every noble thought, every high ideal, every great purpose which has waited through the weary years. And then, as the sap rises in the nation, the men will feel themselves to be the instrument of a newborn national vigour. The special glory of the whole endeavour must be a surge of the whole people's finest qualities worthy to be the prayer: "Let God arise and let His enemies be scattered." '

Thus the stirring cry of David, Israel's warrior king again rang forth as the nation prepared for the greatest military adventure ever undertaken by the race in all its long history.

The Sword of Justice

After asserting that 'among the races of fighting men the British soldier is superb,' General Montgomery added:

'A special gallantry is required of our soldiers. . . . If necessary, we have got to hazard all, and give our lives, that others may enjoy it. From a consecrated nation such men will abundantly come, and "the Lord mighty in battle" will go forth with our armies and His special providence will assist our battle.'

Israel was, in fact, such a consecrated nation—at Sinai they were set apart as a 'peculiar people' hallowed in the service of God (*Exodus* 19:5, 6). But despite their willing acquiescence to God's injunction to obey Him and keep His laws (vs. 7, 8), they eventually turned aside from Him and in consequence were driven from their land and scattered abroad. In modern times the Anglo-Saxon nations have been blindly fulfilling Israel's task. Were they but wholly consecrated in His service they would the more fully undertake their God-given mission and responsibility.

General Montgomery revealed an understanding of this mission when he continued:

'The substance of the tide which has to turn and flow is quite clear. It is not a personal fad or a one-man doctrine. It is the tide which has borne the nation through its history. It is found in the Coronation Service of our King and Queen. The nation's Church handed to our King from the altar of Westminster Abbey the Sword of State: "With this sword do justice, stop the growth of iniquity." The task now in hand is the use of His Majesty's consecrated sword in the re-awakened spirit of that day.'

This charge, delivered by the Archbishop, assuredly bears the imprint of Israel's mission (*Isaiah* 58:6, 7); for, after the exhortation to 'do justice and stop the growth of iniquity,' the Archbishop continues, 'restore the things that are gone into decay, maintain the things that are restored, punish and reform what is amiss, and confirm that which is in good order.' The Sword of State is symbolic also of the sword used by the Rider on the white horse who goes forth in righteousness to 'judge and make war' against the aggressor (*Revelation* 19:11, 19). Furthermore, the sword in the hand of the Lord is repeatedly mentioned in the Scriptures; as for example *Jeremiah* 25:31 and *Isaiah* 66:15, 16.

It is well to recall that Gideon, one of the earliest Israel leaders, when faced with what was, humanly speaking, a vastly superior foe, led his men to victory with the battle cry: 'The sword of the Lord, and of Gideon' (*Judges* 7:18). Note that their own arms were secondary; the sword of the Lord, their spiritual armour, came first. Likewise, before the Battle of El Alamein, General Montgomery spared neither himself nor his men to ensure that every possible human preparation was made; yet, as he reminded his listeners at the Mansion House, he sent his eve of battle message to all ranks: 'Let us pray that the Lord, mighty in battle, will give us the victory.' As a result the Eighth Army was soon known as 'the victorious Desert Army.' Neither did General Montgomery omit to return thanks to God for the victories: in his 1943 Christmas message to the Forces under his command he quoted his former words and added: 'He has done so, and I know that you will agree with me when I say that we must not forget to thank Him for His mercy.'

'An Instrument for Fulfilling His High Purpose'

How truly our beloved and godly King George VI recognized our mission was revealed in the solemn call to prayer and dedication which he broadcast on the evening of D-Day. He said:

'Four years ago our nation and Empire stood alone against an overwhelming enemy, with our backs to the wall. Tested as never before in our history, in God's providence we survived that test; the spirit of the people, resolute, dedicated, burned like a bright flame, lit surely from those Unseen Fires which nothing can quench.

'Now once more a supreme test has to be faced. This time the challenge is not to fight to survive but to fight to win the final victory for the good cause. . . .

'That we may be worthily matched with this new summons of destiny, I desire solemnly to call my people to prayer and dedication.

'We are not unmindful of our own shortcomings, past and present. We shall ask not that God may do our will, but that we may be enabled to do the will of God; and WE DARE TO BELIEVE THAT GOD HAS USED OUR NATION AND EMPIRE AS AN INSTRUMENT FOR FULFILLING HIS HIGH PURPOSE.'

The Consecration of the Armies

Meanwhile, as the physical preparations for invasion proceeded, the chaplains set about their task of preparing the fighting forces spiritually—the culmination of this task being the actual services of dedication held on the eve of D-Day. Press and radio reported many such incidents; for example, Guy Byam, in a B.B.C. war report, gave his personal account of the exploits of paratroops thus:

'We are back into France. Just after midnight I jumped into action with Allied paratroops, the first Allied correspondent to set foot back on French soil. It started on an airfield where the paratroops knelt round their padre in prayer before emplaning. With bent heads and on one knee the men with their equipment and camouflaged faces looked like some strange creatures from another world.'

Thus was obeyed the injunction contained in the Law of the Lord:

'When you set out to make war upon your enemies, and see. . . . an army larger than yourselves, you must not be afraid of them, for the Eternal your God Who brought you out of the land of Egypt is on your side. When you open the campaign, a priest must approach and address the army thus: "Listen, Israel, you are opening a campaign today against your enemies; never lose heart, fear not, tremble not, be not afraid of them, for the Eternal your God goes with you, to fight for you against your enemies and to give you the victory" ' (*Deuteronomy* 20:1-4, Moffatt).

In an uplifting broadcast, 'The Consecration of our Armies,' made shortly after the Normandy landings, the Rev. Canon F. Llewellyn Hughes, Deputy Chaplain-General, said:

'There have been crowded pre-battle Services everywhere; but the consecration of our armies has not been a last-minute effort. It has been a long, laborious process. We aimed at a permanent attitude of mind, at giving to soldiers such a vision of God's Will as would make the doing of it their main purpose. . . .

'As you read incident after incident, comradeship, self-sacrifice and humour, will you weigh my evidence, as General Montgomery's chief padre, that many, many thousands of them went forth for righteousness' sake, and for no other reason. They were not brought to battle by doctored propaganda. The chaplains were never asked to harness the Christian Faith to military operations. Militant ranting was much disliked. We were asked, and strongly asked, to make our men as Christian as we could, to preach the Word of Christ faithfully, because it is true; to minister the sacraments for their own proper effects; to bring men to God that He might make them good.

'The leaders of the invasion force wished most of all that God should impart His own life and desires to the men, and they were certain that then the army would have a sound and honest heart, would hate evil and love good, and go upon this liberating enterprise with a free and genuine enthusiasm.

'Packed into the strange craft the soldiers looked a rough lot. The songs, the banter, and the jokes did not suggest religion. Indeed, most of the men are not regular church-going men; but they are God-going men, and they have their picture of the King of kings in the sanctuary of their hearts. And when General Eisenhower and General Montgomery in their final Orders of the Day asked us all to pray that God would prosper us, that prayer went up, and went up from honest hearts freely and fully convinced that the business in hand was a liberation according to the Will of God.. . . The consecration of an army cannot be completed without the help of the nation whose army we are. There must come to us from the home base not only food, supplies and munitions for the fighting, but also inspiration for the men who fight.

'It is not enough for an army or a nation to have a vague faith in God. It is not enough for us to rest content that our commanders are godly, and that God's flag is publicly flown. Faith in God is useless until it governs action. What does God want done? We believe in God—as what? As a nonentity, content to be recognized, and then ignored? As a vague power, meaningless, purposeless, inarticulate, and therefore unfit to command a platoon, let alone a world? No. We believe in God Who wants, and means to have done, all that Christ embodied, taught, lived out. Let an army and a people learn what God stands for, and then they will know when they are for or against His purpose, and support or oppose with confidence as His commissioned servants. That is where the solid toil of consecration comes in. The character of Christ must be known; His goodness perceived and loved, Himself accepted as Master. No special effort thrown off in an emergency will accomplish that; and there is no short cut.

'So the chaplains are going forward with the forces preaching the simple Gospel of Christ, the Author and Finisher of all the fine qualities of men. . . .

'There is no ideal of character better than the one God sent to us in Jesus Christ our Lord. Read the New Testament again, check up all that moves in you by His standards, and so make Him the Light and Guide of your day's work. It is not a little, narrow, personal matter; it is the one, big, corporate movement in which every man, woman and child can take a part. Christ's Spirit in every man is God's simple, but masterly and scientific, scheme for making the whole body of the world sound by making healthy every cell in it. . . .

'I ask you to join the long, laborious, but most happy process of reconsecration, and to pray that God's love may go forth in us conquering and to conquer, that we may bear in our midst a Light of Hope indeed to the waiting peoples, and that all nations may see in the conduct of our battle the might of our cause, and in the conduct of our men the good for whose enthronement we have fought. . . .'

Knights' Vigil

It has since been revealed that an historic service was held on Sunday, June 4, forty-eight hours before the invasion of Normandy. A reporter wrote in the *Sunday Express* (28.3.48):

'General Sir Miles Dempsey, who commanded the British Second Army in the invasion of Europe, told me today the four-year-old secret of one of the most historic and dramatic religious services ever held.

'It will be commemorated on June 6 this year, fourth anniversary of D-Day, by the unveiling of stained glass windows—depicting the warrior saints, St. Michael and St. George, tanks, guns and landing craft—at Portsdown Parish Church, where the service was held. This 70-year-old parish church overlooks the road down which the Allied forces trooped 24 hours later to the invasion ships.

'The idea of a Knights' Vigil, as on battle eve in olden days, came from the Rev. J.W. J. Steele, then Assistant Chaplain-General of the Second Army. "It was one of the most moving experiences of my life," said General Dempsey. The vigil lasted an hour. The church was filled by 400 officers and men of Second Army H.Q. staff.

'With military police guarding the doors and the Allied armies poised in sealed camps in the surrounding woods, the chaplain recited the famous prayer Drake offered before Cadiz in 1587: "O Lord God, when Thou givest to Thy servants to endeavour any great matter, grant us also to know that it is not the beginning, but the continuing of the same, until it be thoroughly finished, which yieldeth the true glory; through Him that for the finishing of Thy work laid down His life, our Redeemer, Jesus Christ."

'The sunshine of the morning gave way to storm clouds as the planners of D-Day answered this solemn call to service: "To the Second Army there has been given a glorious part in a great task. To relieve the oppressed, to restore freedom in Europe, and to bring peace to the world. As we stand upon the threshold of the greatest adventure in our history, let us now offer to Almighty God all our powers of body, mind, and spirit, so that our great endeavour may be thoroughly finished. To this end, will you undertake the heavy responsibility that such a task places upon each of you, and with God's help carry it through, giving of the best, until Victory is won and Peace assured?"

'Four hundred voices responded, "I will, the Lord being helper." Then came the Blessing: "Go forth into action with a stout heart: be of good courage: hold fast that which is good: render to no man evil for evil: strengthen the faint-hearted: support the weak: help the afflicted: honour all men: love and serve the Lord, rejoicing in the power of God with us."

'The Miracle of D-Day'

An account of this most fateful operation of the war was given in a *Daily Telegraph* (7.4.47) article, 'The Miracle of D-Day,' by Lt. Gen. Sir Frederick Morgan, who was head of the British and American Planning Staff preparing for invasion. General Morgan wrote:

'As the old, almost forgotten adage had it, "Man proposes but God disposes." There comes a point in so many of our affairs at which, when we have done everything of which we are capable, there remains no more but to leave it all. . . . We hope so often for a miracle.

'And miracles happen still. How many of them have we not seen enacted before our very eyes in these past few years. The history of them is now in the writing, and when we come to read it I sometimes wonder how the attribution of success will be worked out.

'There was Dunkirk and its flat calm sea. Who planned that? During those fateful hours I was riding up to battle, south of the Somme River, with my divisional commander in his armoured command vehicle, to do what could be done with our small resources to create some diversion to the relief of our main army which, we knew, was very hemmed in on those northern beaches. There were many others who, like us, saw no way out, barring a miracle. There came a miracle.

'Then, two years later, in Gen. Eisenhower's rear Headquarters at Norfolk House in London, how intently we watched the charts which showed us the convoys in their tortuous progress from the United States and from Britain to make the landings in North Africa. At the same time, those charts showed us the location and movement of every enemy submarine marauding in the Atlantic. Partly by design, of course, there was no contact between submarine and convoy. But there was a breath-taking moment when a U-boat caught sight of the tail ship of one convoy, the rest being obscured in a squall that seemed to be travelling with our ships. The German observer, apparently, thought what he saw merely worthy of routine report.

'Then, but a day before Gen. Patton was due to land on the Casablanca beaches, open to the full Atlantic swell, just as it seemed inevitable that his whole affair must be called off, the wind changed from on-shore to off-shore and let the small craft in. There was surely more than planning here too.

'The history of our other theatres of war will inevitably tell of many similar happenings, but I doubt if any will be such as to compare with the miracle of D-Day in 1944, when our troops from Britain set foot once more in France and opened the last campaign against Germany.

'. . . Every hazard that could be eliminated had been eliminated. Every foreseeable risk had been covered, and then came that weather.

'. . . All culminated at a terrific moment when Gen. Eisenhower, the Supreme Commander, gave his fateful decision that the attack be launched across the Channel, which at that moment, looked as forbidding as only our

Channel can look. Seldom can one man have been faced with the making of a decision so critical. Had he decided otherwise than he did, there was abundant evidence existing to support a negative decision. Had he decided otherwise this would never have been written, not in English anyway, for had the attack not been made when it was made, there is every possibility that it might never have been made at all.

'There had already been one short delay, caused by bad weather, which meant that any further postponement must have been of weeks to await the next conjunction of light and tide such as the assault plan envisaged. Radical alteration of assault technique to admit of attack under a different set of circumstances of tide and light would have been virtually an impossibility in any space of time that could be accepted.

'Already, and how understandably, the strain was beginning visibly to tell on all ranks, from the men who were actually to do the desperate job to those on whom the major responsibility rested. The full possible reaction of an anti-climax such as long delay would have caused was incalculable. But what could be foreseen clearly was that the secret of it all, hitherto, once more by a miraculous combination of good management and good luck, immaculately guarded, would certainly be broken. Too many people now knew too much, since all were fully briefed for the part each had to play.

'Had the enemy known just what was coming to him his counter measures could have been effective. Had our assault failed he would have created for himself the opportunity to perfect all those "secret weapons" that we know now, as we did not know then, were in the making.

'There was no immediate alternative open to us, should our first onset have failed for any reason to materialize or to succeed. There were no spare resources in many of our key items of provision should casualties have exceeded estimates and, in such an affair, estimates must by the nature of things be high.

'As it was, at the Supreme Commander's word there set out a combined American and British Navy and Army and Air Force in which every individual, or so it seemed, had no thought in his mind but of success. Somehow it all seemed inevitable to everyone.

'None took counsel of their fears, for, in truth, the contemplation of failure would have been more than could be borne. So fears were set aside and off went the ships and the aircraft and their men into the unknown, certain of victory.

'There was something more than ordinary, surely, both in that decision to attack and in that spirit of success that permeated the ranks.'

D-Day Weather

The gravity of the decision which General Eisenhower was forced to make is revealed in the following editorial comment in *The Times* (11.9.44):

'The whole meteorological episode has provided interesting reading for those who spent their days at the time tapping barometers in a fever of anxiety and looking out of the window every five minutes to see whether the wind was treating the trees less boisterously and the clouds were giving a less impressive imitation of November storms. . . .

'It seemed that those normally placid and sunlit days when May and June mingle were this summer malignantly possessed. . . . And yet all the time, had we but known it, the clouds we so much dreaded were big with opportunities Supreme Headquarters were quick to grasp. The weather, indeed while we were able to probe its secrets, bluffed the enemy completely for, in the words of the report:

'"The German commanders were advised by their meteorological service that there could be no invasion in the period including June 6 because of continuous stormy weather. That is why D-Day forces landing during a brief break in the windiest month in Normandy for at least 20 years found so many

German troops without officers, and why other enemy coastal units were having exercises at the time of the landings."

'That the onlooker sees most of the game is one of those half-truths which, in the final analysis, are so misleading. . . . It is not, however, always given to him correctly to interpret what he sees, and the weather, which has so often deserved all that is said of it, certainly deserves apologies for the imprecations it came in for at the time of the landings.'

The official story of the invasion weather forecast, reported in *The Times* (2.9.44), is of great interest because it reveals that in spite of the very long odds against completely unfavourable conditions prevailing, the weather after all gave true cause for thanksgiving:

'For months the meteorological section at Supreme Headquarters had been studying the relative advantages of May, June and July for weather. Using statistics, they found that the chances were about 50 to 1 against weather, tide, and moon being favourable for all services, land, sea and air. . . .

'When the commanders' final series of meetings began on Thursday, June 1, the first indication was given that conditions in the Channel on the Monday were unlikely to meet even the minimum requirements. . . . In the early hours of Sunday morning the Supreme Commander postponed the biggest military operation in history on a day-to-day basis. Late in the evening of Sunday there was fairly strong evidence that after a stormy Monday there would be a temporary improvement overnight, and for the greater part of Tuesday. By now the weather in the Atlantic was more like mid-winter than early June. Any improvement on Tuesday would be short-lived. The assault could not take place on the Wednesday, because some of the naval forces from the more distant embarkation ports had set out in advance of the final decision and would need to return to port if the assault was deferred beyond Tuesday. . .

'At a full meeting of the Supreme Commander and his staff late on Sunday evening his meteorological advisers presented this historic forecast:

'"An interval of fair conditions will spread throughout the Channel area on Monday and last until at least dawn on Tuesday, June 6. Winds will fall to Force 3 or 4 on the Normandy coasts and cloud will be well broken with a base height of about 3,000 feet. After that interval it will become cloudy or overcast again during Tuesday afternoon. Then, following a brief fair interval on Tuesday night or early Wednesday, conditions will continue variable with indeterminate periods of overcast skies and fresh winds until Friday."

'Shortly afterwards the Supreme Commander said that he had provisionally decided that the invasion should go forward on Tuesday morning. The Supreme Commander, his Commander-in-Chief, and their chiefs of staff met again at 4 am on Monday for "the final and irrevocable decision." Shortly afterwards messages went to all the vast forces concerned. The invasion of France would start on the morning of the next day.

'On the morning of the assault the wind had moderated, and the cloud was not only well broken, but its base was at least 4,000 feet high, ideally suited for the large-scale airborne operations. In the hour preceding the landings, when perfect conditions for pinpoint bombing were so essential, there were large areas of temporarily clear sky, and throughout the critical time medium and light bombers were unhampered.'

Thus God had kept His promise, 'O Israel, Fear not. . . . when thou passest through the waters, I will be with thee' (*Isaiah* 43:1, 2).

The wisdom of General Eisenhower's decision was emphasized still more by a further article in *The Times* (27.10.44):

'It has perhaps never been fully appreciated how near the invasion forces came to a disaster comparable with the fate of the Spanish Armada. Rear-Admiral William Tennant, who directed the construction off the Normandy beaches of the astonishing prefabricated harbours, said: "Those of us who were embarked and waiting in the assault ships remember how D-Day had already been postponed for twenty-four hours on account of bad weather. Had it been put off for a day more the expedition would probably have been delayed until June 18, the earliest day of propitious tides. Sunday, June 18, Admiral Tennant reminded us, was a perfect summer evening on the Channel. His staff had taken the opportunity of fair weather to sail across twenty-three tows of pier equipment for the harbours. The Forecast was good, yet only one of these tows survived. At four o'clock the next morning the gale began and became steadily worse for twenty-four hours before it moderated and died away after two and a half days. Had the invasion fleet come in on that Sunday, as could easily have happened, the whole expedition might have been wrecked.'

Who gave General Eisenhower the wisdom after the first delay of twenty-four hours to decide against further postponement to a later, and as it turned out, far less favourable date? Was it not God? Speaking in his home town, Abilene, Kansas, on June 4, 1952, he is reported in *Time* (16.6.52) to have said 'with an intent and distant look across his face:'

'This day eight years ago, I made the most agonising decision of my life. I had to decide to postpone by at least twenty-four hours the most formidable array of fighting ships and of fighting men that was ever launched across the sea against a hostile shore. The consequences of that decision at that moment could not have been foreseen by anyone. If there were nothing else in my life to prove the existence of an almighty and merciful God, the events of the next twenty-four hours did it. . . . The greatest break in a terrible outlay of weather occurred the next day and allowed that great invasion to proceed, with losses far below those we had anticipated. . . .'

The Rainbow of Invasion Morning

Since the days of Noah the rainbow has been a sign in remembrance of God's judgment upon the wicked and His promise of future mercy. It is therefore of interest that features of the shoulder flash worn by officers and personnel attached to Supreme Headquarters Allied Expeditionary Force are a rainbow and a sword. This badge is described in *The Sunday Times* (26.3.44):

'The shield-shaped cloth patch with a black background, representing the darkness of Nazi oppression, bears the Crusader's sword of liberation with the red flames of avenging justice leaping from its hilt. Above the sword is a rainbow, emblematic of hope, containing all the colours of which Allied flags are composed.'

In a most singular manner, the rainbow was further associated with the Invasion Forces when on D-Day, as the combined British and United States Army of Liberation landed on the beaches of Normandy, a magnificent bow was arched over the battle area. The following account of the phenomenon was given in *The Sphere* (24.6.44):

'Lately there has been talk in some parts of the country about signs in the sky. The one depicted by our artist in this drawing was witnessed over the Invasion area at dawn on D-Day. The rainbow spread right across the combat zone in brilliant colours, only fading from sight after thousands of our men had seen it and been heartened by its appearance at the outset of the Great Adventure. One aeroplane crew reported that they had flown through the middle of it whilst carrying out a bombing mission over the beaches. "It stood out as plain as could be. I watched it for quite a while," said the aircraft's turret gunner. Below him at that moment was the whole panorama of the Invasion, with vessels crowding in on the beaches, gun-flashes and bomb-bursts all along the coast and fleets of aircraft flying over to cover the ground forces. Coming at the precise moment when it did, the Rainbow of Invasion Morn might rank with the Angels of Mons of the last war. . . .'

This sign in the heavens at such a time was surely a confirmation that the Almighty's blessing rested upon the cause of 'setting the captives free,' to which the Anglo-Saxon peoples, as partners in this Great Crusade, were committed. It also serves as a most pointed reminder that, because of their Redeemer, God has promised that He will establish His people in righteousness and peace and that He has given assurance that no weapon, secret or otherwise, shall prosper against them:

'For a small moment have I forsaken thee; but with great mercies will I gather thee. In a little wrath I hid My face from thee for a moment; but with everlasting kindness will I have mercy on thee, saith the Lord thy Redeemer. For this is as the waters of Noah unto Me: for as I have sworn that the waters of Noah should no more go over the earth; so have I sworn that I would not be wroth with thee, nor rebuke thee. For the mountains shall depart, and the hills be removed; but My kindness shall not depart from thee, neither shall the covenant of My peace be removed, saith the Lord that hath mercy on thee. . . .

'In righteousness shalt thou be established: thou shall be far from oppression; for thou shalt not fear: and from terror; for it shall not come near thee. . . . No weapon that is formed against thee shall prosper; and every tongue that shall rise against thee in judgment thou shalt condemn. This is the heritage of the servants of the Lord, and their righteousness is of Me, saith the Lord' (*Isaiah* 54:7-10, 14, 17).

God did indeed answer the prayers which were offered up to Him, prospering and preserving the Invasion Armies, yet there was a tendency, as is clearly revealed in some recently published memoirs, for certain generals to succumb to the temptation, despite God's forewarning 'that Israel might glory over Him by claiming, "My own hand has won the victory"' (*Judges* 7:2, Moffatt), instead of following the example of General Montgomery who, in a message to his armies after the triumphant advance through France, said: 'Such an historic march of events can seldom have taken place in such a short space of time. . . . Let us say to each other, "This was the Lord's doing, and it is marvellous in our eyes".'

The tragedy of Arnhem, when the weather was persistently unfavourable to the British and American Airborne Forces, and the German breakthrough in the Ardennes in the winter of 1944, revealed the folly of relying upon carefully laid plans or material strength. Among other occasions when the weather was favourable to the enemy was April 1941 when persistent fog permitted the German battle cruisers *Scharnhorst* and *Gneisenau* to pass through the Denmark Straits unobserved and carry out successful sorties on

British shipping in the Atlantic, sinking or capturing twenty-two ships amounting to 115,000 tons.

Moreover, the fact that there were many instances of Divine Intervention does not signify that God would give victory without stern fighting and severe setbacks, for absolute and speedy supremacy over all enemies was promised only as a consequence of unfeigned obedience to the Will of God. In days gone by Moses adjured the people of Israel:

'If thou shalt hearken diligently unto the voice of the Lord thy God, to observe and to do all His commandments. . . . The Lord shall cause thine enemies that rise up against thee to be smitten before thy face: they shall come out against thee one way, and flee before thee seven ways. . . . And the Lord shall make thee the head, and not the tail; and thou shalt be above only, and thou shalt not be beneath' (*Deuteronomy* 28:1-13; cf. *Leviticus* 26:3-7).

These conditional promises also provide a clue as to why, although eventually gaining military victory over Nazi Germany, the Western Allies suffered political defeat at the hand of Stalin—facts concerning which are so clearly revealed by Chester Wilmot in *The Struggle for Europe.*

'Why Has God Preserved Us?'

The belief which emerged from the fact that the most critical military and naval operations of the war turned in our favour, when in almost every instance they might by a slight change of circumstances have resulted in a major disaster or even defeat, is summed up by the Bishop of Chelmsford, Dr. H. A. Wilson, in an article, 'Victory is God's Giving,' in the *Sunday Chronicle* (1.4.45):

'If ever a great nation was on the point of supreme and final disaster, and yet was saved and reinstated, it was ourselves. That is a fact which should be written on the souls of us all in indelible letters of fire. It does not require an exceptional religious mind to detect in all this the Hand of God. It has been a miracle and the person who does not recognize that is impervious to the deeper significance of events. We have been saved for a purpose. Let that be acknowledged, and it will be an immense steadying force in our character. OUR EMPIRE HAS A MISSION TO DISCHARGE IN THE WORLD. THAT MAY SOUND OLD FASHIONED AND JINGOISTIC, BUT IT IS TRUE.'

President Truman too believes that the United States has a Divinely appointed mission for in a speech at Washington on April 3, 1951, he averred:

'I do not think that anyone can study the history of this nation of ours without becoming convinced that Divine Providence has played a great part in it.

'I HAVE THE FEELING THAT GOD HAS CREATED US AND BROUGHT US TO OUR PRESENT POSITION OF POWER AND STRENGTH FOR SOME GREAT PURPOSE. It is not given to us now to know fully what that purpose is. But I think we may be sure of one thing. And that is that our country is intended to do all it can, in co-operation with other nations, to help to create peace and preserve peace in the world. It is given to us to defend the spiritual values—the moral code—against the vast forces of evil that seek to destroy them.'

The late Archbishop of Canterbury, Dr. Temple, also held the belief that Britain was saved for a purpose; moreover, he revealed an understanding of what that purpose is when in a sermon at St. Paul's Cathedral on Battle of Britain Sunday, September 26, 1943, he said:

'WHY HAS GOD PRESERVED US? WE MAY, AND WE MUST, BELIEVE THAT HE WHO HAS LED OUR FATHERS IN WAYS SO STRANGE, AND HAS PRESERVED OUR LAND IN A MANNER SO MARVELLOUS, HAS A PURPOSE FOR US TO SERVE IN THE PREPARATION FOR HIS PERFECT KINGDOM. IN THE TRADITION OF OUR NATION AND OUR EMPIRE, WE ARE ENTRUSTED WITH A TREASURE TO BE USED FOR THE WELFARE OF MANKIND' (*Christian World,* 30.9.43).

A Servant People
Can it be that in God's inscrutable Providence Britain is the nation of

whom Christ spoke when He said to the Jews: 'The kingdom of God shall be taken from you, and given to a nation bringing forth the fruits thereof?' (*Matthew* 21:43). Can it be that Britain, together with the British Commonwealth and the United States, is fulfilling the destiny foretold for the descendants of Abraham, 'In thy seed shall all the nations of the earth be blessed' (*Genesis* 26:4) and that they are the 'nation' and 'company of nations' (*Genesis* 35:11) promised to the patriarch's grandson, Jacob-Israel? In any case it is suggestive that despite their preservation by God time and time again when they have called upon Him and honoured His name, the English-speaking peoples remain blind to their vocation and deaf to their high calling.

The words of God through the prophet Isaiah do indeed apply to the British and American peoples:

'Thou, Israel, art My servant, Jacob whom I have chosen, the seed of Abraham My friend. Fear not, thou worm Jacob, and ye men of Israel; I will help thee, saith the Lord, and thy redeemer, the Holy One of Israel' (*Isaiah* 41:8, 14).

'Hear, ye deaf; and look, ye blind, that ye may see. Who is blind, but My servant? or deaf, as My messenger that I sent? who is blind as he that is perfect, and blind as the Lord's servant?' (*Isaiah* 42:18, 19).

'Ye are My witnesses, saith the Lord, and My servant whom I have chosen: that ye may know and believe Me, and understand that I am He: before Me there was no God formed, neither shall there be after Me. I have declared, and have saved, and I have shewed, when there was no strange god among you: therefore ye are My witnesses, saith the Lord, that I am God' (*Isaiah* 43:10, 12).

Lest Ye Forget. . . . Your God

The warning which the Bishop of Chelmsford went on to give regarding the possibility of and dire consequences which would result from refusal to fulfil our vocation was, even while he wrote, being justified by events: before the war ended there were marked signs of an alarming drop in spiritual temperature to which the Bishop of Southwell was moved to direct attention in *The Sunday Times* (22.7.45):

'England stands at the cross-roads of destiny. "When the Lord has given you this good land"—and He has given it to us back again, alive from the dead, out of mortal peril—"then take heed to yourselves lest ye forget the Lord your God." What kind of people do we mean to be? Along what road do we intend to travel? Christian civilization has been given one more chance, and we shall be judged before God and man by the way we use it. Are we to remain a Christian people or are we going to follow the false road of uncreative and sterile materialism?

'That is the biggest question before us all, to which all other questions are secondary. It is not yet certain how we mean to answer it. In many departments of our national life there are ominous warnings of a moral breakdown.'

'Lest ye forget the Lord thy God'! And how speedily did we forget Him! Less than a year later, in a leading article, 'To Whom is the Victory?,' the *Daily Sketch* (5.6.46) was provoked to ask: 'Are we a nation of infidels or "an acceptable people in the sight of God"? Have we no gratitude in our hearts? No faith?'

'It would seem as if uncertain answers would have to be given to each of these important questions.

'On Saturday next, June 8, 1946, this nation will celebrate, in the streets of London, its glorious victory over two great enemies. That dual triumph, whatever unbelievers may hold to the contrary, we believe to be due solely to the mercy of Almighty God. We believe that but for His Divine Intervention we should be fed with the bread of tears, biting the dust in humiliation and degradation. Defeat and all the sorrows that wait on the vanquished would have been our lot.

'Pick up your official programme. Search its twenty pages from end to end. You will find a single reference to God on its front page in the motto of the Kings of England—Dieu et mon droit.

'In the days of our trial, in the dark and terrifying years through which we had to pass, we felt it necessary to organize, throughout the land, twenty-six days and two whole weeks of urgent prayer. We filled our churches with congregations kneeling in genuine devotion and faith to the great Mediator and Advocate, imploring His forgiveness for their sins, pleading for help in our tribulation and the danger of others than ourselves. He responded. He answered our cry. Now that victory has come, we adorn our houses and streets with decorations, make the night brilliant with illuminations. . . . Could we not have spared two minutes for prayer to God?'

The following Sunday, June 9, was not even observed as a Day of Thanksgiving to God. It is noteworthy, however, that, as always, Their Majesties King George VI and Queen Elizabeth, set an example to the nation by attending Divine Service at Westminster Abbey. Many of their subjects also returned thanks, but the masses were unmindful of God and the great deliverances He had vouchsafed.

So Britain forgot the Lord her God, as did Israel of old whom God admonishes through prophet and psalmist:

'Thou has forgotten the God of thy salvation, and hast not been mindful of the rock of thy strength.'
'They (Israel) soon forgat His works (deliverance from their enemies); they waited not for His counsel.'
'Thou has forgotten Me, and trusted in falsehood.'
'They have perverted their way, and they have forgotten the Lord their God.'

The consequences of Israel's neglect of God, so graphically recorded by

Old Testament writers, were economic disaster, moral decline and defeat at the hand of her enemies.

At this point, here are more events revealing the Hand of God

More evidence of the providential working of God in the lives of His people has come to light since this book was last published. There are doubtless many more events and situations which could be included but the following three are included here to show that there is always more to be discovered.

Atomic Judgment on Japan . . . and the Preservation of the Host

If atomic weapons had not been used on Japan in 1945, the likelihood was that both the United States and Japan would have resorted to chemical and biological weapons. Only a weapon of inconceivable novelty and power was capable of bringing about an unconditional Japanese surrender. The Japanese look upon fire as a 'god.' On August 6 and 9, 1945, their god appeared on earth and lived among them. The god that answered by fire *was God* and the nation of Japan under their Emperor-god surrendered. The cities of Hiroshima and Nagasaki are printed in the historical record.

What is not generally known is that Nagasaki was not a primary target and here a very powerful postscript testimony to over-ruling Divine Intervention was contained in a radio broadcast in America by Paul Harvey, on Sunday evening, December 13, 1953. This is what he said in part:

'It was out there somewhere from an island named Guam that one of our then mightiest bombers took off—a B-29. Another swift deadly arrow of destruction was on its way—the target, Japan.

'The sleek bomber turned in a lazy arc above the cloud that shrouded the target, making three runs over the city in fifty-five minutes—until the gas supply would not stand for more of this. It seemed a shame to be right over the primary target of Kokura and then pass it up, but there was no choice. That strange cloud, almost like an omen, which said, "this city must be spared." With one more puzzled look back, the crew headed for the secondary target. The sky was clear—"bombs away!"—and the B-29 hightailed it for home.

'Weeks later Major Sweeney received information from military intelligence which made his blood run cold. Allied prisoners of war, thousands of them, the biggest concentration of imprisoned Americans in enemy hands, had been moved on August 1 to a town named Kokura. "Thank God," breathed the skipper, "thank God for that cloud."

'Yes, the city which was hidden from our bomber that August 9, 1945 was a prison camp and thousands of Americans are now alive who would have died but for that unexplained cloud which rolled in from the sea. You see the secondary target that day was Nagasaki and the missile intended for Kokura was the world's second atomic bomb.'

It was the Psalmist who declared of the LORD, *"He spread a cloud for a covering"* (*Psalm* 105:39). The covering of a cloud for the American prisoners was the promised protection for the host of Israel which were not forgotten by Jehovah as the atomic fire was about to fall around them. The B-29 circled in the sky like an angel of death three times in fifty-five minutes, confirming the Three Persons of the Godhead with five as the number of grace and Redemption. The covering was as sure as that for His people in Egypt long ago when judgment passed through the land where Israel was in bondage.

'Operation Esther'

On November 11, 1965, Rhodesia made a Unilateral Declaration of Independence at 11.15 am. As it was the anniversary of the Armistice in 1918, the dramatic event was timed specifically not to coincide with the same 11th hour of the cessation of hostilities in the Great War.

Mr Ian Smith, the Prime Minister, on the eve of UDI, passed down the line of his assembled Cabinet members asking each one in turn if they supported what was about to happen. When he came to Mr. Richard Hall (who years later became Secretary to the British-Israel-World Federation in England) he received an affirmative response, but was urged by Hall to hold a day of prayer.

The story of UDI in Rhodesia is remarkable and even miraculous in respect of the faith of its white Christian community and of the Guardian of its people. This small land-locked country held out for 14 years in a terrorist war against the forces of Communism and the new internationalist and mostly paganised world.

In February 1966 sanctions were imposed against Rhodesia by the United Nations, which forged a breed of people who had to travel the world under various cloaks and disguises to break sanctions so that a small beleaguered country could survive.

Then in 1978, after six years of what was known as the 'Bush War' and as the intensity of this turmoil and terrorism in Rhodesia steadily increased, God raised up a mighty army of women in hundreds who called themselves, 'Operation Esther.' It was based on the story of Esther in the Old Testament (or Covenant) who prayed with all fervency before the Lord God of Israel to deliver her people from the hand of the wicked.

Mrs Claudette Gradwell and her two companions, Mrs Judith Copeland and Mrs Kathy Symington began the prayer movement in Salisbury. These women were unknown to Mrs Elvin Hitchcock who about the same time started the prayer movement in Bulawayo. A number of farming families, who were constantly within the orbit of Operation Esther, had to remain anonymous.

It happened many times that 'The Esthers' would communicate across the country and pray immediately when they heard that the people on the farms were under attack. Sometimes even without knowing of the attack they would feel the burden for people and pray for deliverance which did indeed take place. Just three of many accounts must suffice here.

In September 1978, Vincent and Sarah, with their two daughters and son left their farm house in the Mrewa area for Salisbury airport to meet parents flying in from Britain via Johannesburg. Just before they left, Sarah, having come across a letter from the Esther Group in Salisbury, on impulse picked up the telephone and asked for prayer. Unusually the call was put through immediately (it could sometimes take up to 30 minutes) to hear that the group were meeting within half an hour and would pray.

On the road they were ambushed; their Landrover was immobilised and set on fire. They were pinned down by raking fire from around seven guerrilla terrorists. In a desperate bid to divert fire from his family, Vincent, rose to his full height, bounded away to the left and towards the guerrillas in a suicidal charge fully expecting to die. In his mind and in a final plea crying out 'O God, help us, God help us.' He saw the weapons leap in the hands of two terrorists as they fired—but they were not firing in his direction. They were moving back, crouching as they did so, aiming their weapons at targets well away from Vincent until they were out of sight when amazingly the shooting stopped. The family were all safe and uninjured when picked up three hours later by a passing delivery truck.

Two weeks later a captured guerrilla in the Lomagundi area admitted to being one of the group which attacked Vincent's Landrover. He said they had run back into the bush and made for rougher country when they saw 'a lot of people running towards them, some riding on horses.' The prayers for the safety of the family had been answered.

1979 was a year of many tragedies throughout the country, but also of miracles. There was an elderly couple, Charles and Alice, who came under attack on their farm in August. With no way of protecting themselves they knelt down and prayed. Just when the terrorists were closing in and increasing their fire, the shooting suddenly stopped. The attackers fled and disappeared into the bush.

Sometime later a security force patrol in the area engaged and captured some of the guerrillas who had attacked the farm house. The leader told his captors that just as they were advancing from their positions, 'We saw many people coming out of the house and running towards us. We did not know how many people there were but there were many. They kept running towards us. We became very frightened and ran away.'

It was not only the white Rhodesians who experienced this kind of miracle. In June 1979 a small patrol of young black servicemen was in one of the eastern tribal trust lands and was ambushed being seriously outnumbered. It was led by Sgt Manangwe who had accepted Christianity from his mission school days in Mashonaland. In desperation he called on his men to pray saying 'Help us God, help us through your Son, Jesus Christ, Christ save us.' Within seconds or minutes the terrorist firing stopped. When they eventually got to the ambush positions there was not trace of them except for empty cartridges. They calculated that there must have been eighteen or twenty men against their seven.

About a week later two of the guerrillas who had set up the ambush were captured. When questioned by Sgt Manangwe as to why they had broken off the engagement when they had the advantage, they said that they had stopped firing and decided to get out of their position as fast as possible because of the reinforcements they saw coming up behind them. There were no reinforcements and not a soul came to assist the patrol that day.

Operation Esther succeeded in that it showed once again the power, the awesome power, of prayer. Rhodesia changed to Zimbabwe and many of the colonial names of cities, towns and villages disappeared into the pages of history as indeed did the foundation of its peace. It would appear that the Guardian of that former country left with its people.

The Falklands War
The following extract is taken from Margaret Thatcher *The Downing Street Years* (1993), pp173-85:

'The significance of the Falklands War was enormous, both for Britain's self-confidence and for our standing in the world. Since the Suez fiasco in 1956, British foreign policy had been one long retreat. The tacit assumption made by British and foreign governments alike was that our world role was doomed steadily to diminish. We had come to be seen by both friends and enemies as a nation which lacked the will and the capability to defend its interests in peace, let alone in war. Victory in the Falklands changed that. Everywhere I went after the war, Britain's name meant something more than it had. The war also had real importance in relations between East and West: years later I was told by a Russian general that the Soviets had been firmly convinced that we would not fight for the Falklands, and that if we did fight we would lose. We proved them wrong on both counts, and they did not forget the fact. ...'

On the evening of March 31, 1982, with the Argentinian invasion fleet already at sea off the Falkland Islands, Prime Minister Margaret Thatcher was in her room at the House of Commons in a meeting with the Secretary of State for Defence, Sir John Nott, discussing what if anything could be done to retake the Falklands. The Foreign Secretary and the Chief of the Defence Staff were out of the country. Nott gave the Ministry of Defence view that the Falklands could not be retaken once they were seized. Depression was descending on the meeting when the First Sea Lord, Sir Henry Leach, arrived late to brush aside the serious doubts of the MOD (Comedy had intervened as in civilian dress he had been delayed getting through security and had to be rescued from being detained by police in the Central Lobby of the House of Commons).

The Chief of the Naval Staff was asked if retaking the islands was possible, he replied *'Yes, we can recover the islands.'* He then added *'and we must!'* Thatcher's retort was *'Why do you say that?'* Sir Henry replied *"because if we don't do that, in a few months we will be living in a different country whose word will count for little!'* He said a Task Force could be ready to leave in forty-eight hours. This was greeted by the Prime Minister with relief and approval, who then proceeded to give the order to retake the

Falklands. With Leach being at the end of his career, the timing that year was critical.

The Falklands campaign was successful, in no small part, thanks to Sir Henry Leach, among others, and he was appointed Admiral of the Fleet when he retired from active service at the end of 1982. He was the right man in the right place at the right time—and undoubtedly also was the woman, Margaret Thatcher. There are many recorded instances where critical timing has proved to be the over-ruling Providence in Britain's victory against the aggressor. In the case of the Falklands conflict, the Vulcan bomber was only ninety days away from being scrapped, yet it performed a key role over the longest-range air attack in history. Britain's two aircraft carriers also came through the conflict unscathed, the weather intervening to keep Argentinian aircraft grounded at critical points preventing attacks on the carriers.

One of the most striking aspects of Operation CORPORATE (the codename given to the British operation to retake the Falklands) was the relationship between the three Services. Relations were always good, reflecting a widely held view of a very real sense of unified action. There was very close co-operation with all three, including the various secretariats, especially concerning procurement and planning.

The story of RAF command and control for the operation is essentially one of improvisation. It quickly became apparent that the normal RAF pattern of command and control was not fitted to the highly unusual requirements of Operation CORPORATE; instead a system had to be improvised as the operation unfolded and further roles added. That it worked is a tribute to the ability of individuals to adapt themselves and their aircraft to a special situation and to the sense that a guiding hand was present throughout.

Just three months before the conflict cuts in Naval defence were announced. The cut back in defence spending followed immediately by the demands of unanticipated conflict is a continuing story right up to the present day. Thankfully so also is the over-ruling Providence of our Guardian.

'We Looked for Peace . . . and Behold Trouble'

Britain, and indeed all the English-speaking peoples, now find themselves in a sorry plight. 'We looked for peace, and there is no good; and for the time of healing, and behold trouble!' (*Jeremiah* 14:19). This cry of God's people of old has a familiar ring today, for it reflects the feeling of bitter frustration which is the experience of the people of Britain and to some degree also the peoples of the Commonwealth and the United States.

The English-speaking people looked for peace but instead they are faced with world-wide unrest and strife. They are again involved in war, and over the whole globe there is the ominous threat of aggression waged with terrible atomic and bacteriological weapons. Although they may take comfort in the promise, 'No weapon forged against you shall succeed, no tongue raised against you shall win its plea. Such is the lot of the Eternal's servants; thus, the Eternal promises, do I maintain their cause' (*Isaiah* 54:17, Moffatt), they should honestly examine their present state and make sure that they are still truly God's servants and that they seek His righteousness.

The people of Britain hoped for recovery from the ravages of war and the attainment of a higher standard of living, but instead they have had to face continuing austerity and one economic crisis after another. Now to add to their difficulties they have had to shoulder the crushing burden of a vast re-armament programme.

The plaint of Jeremiah was, 'O Lord, though our iniquities testify against us, do Thou it for Thy name's sake: for our back-slidings are many; we have sinned against Thee. O the hope of Israel, the saviour thereof in time of trouble, why shouldest Thou be as a stranger in the land, and as a wayfaring man that turneth aside to tarry for a night?' (14:7, 8). Are not our backslidings many? Is not God a stranger in the land today? Nationally we sought Him during the war but now we are shunning Him and making the Hope of Israel a stranger and a wayfarer.

Over several decades false prophets have prophesied lies, painting rosy pictures of a brave new world in which it was suggested that smaller effort would command greater reward, but their visions are now revealed as a deception and a lie. They refused to face the fact that the decree which God made known to Adam has not yet been annulled: 'In the sweat of thy face shalt thou eat bread' (*Genesis* 3:19). No man, no nation, may infringe the Divine fiat with impunity. All too late there was coined the much criticized slogan, 'Work or Want.'

'Remember . . . He that Giveth Thee Power to Get Wealth'

Moreover, the planners of Britain's post-war Utopia based their schemes for post-war reconstruction on purely material considerations, and encouraged the people to say in their hearts: 'My power and the might of mine hand hath gotten me this wealth' (*Deuteronomy* 8:17). The acuteness of our present plight is a direct result of national forgetfulness of God and disregard of the injunction: 'Thou shalt remember the Lord thy God: for it is He that giveth thee power to get wealth, that He may establish His covenant which He swore unto thy fathers. . . .' (v.18). A clause of that covenant was that God's people should be a blessing to all the nations of the earth and to that end they were promised great riches and power. Why is Britain's position as a world power declining? Why is she relinquishing her overseas commitments and responsibilities? The answer is that she can only fulfil her task of leadership as God's servant nation if He, the source of her wealth, is honoured, believed and obeyed.

How lamentably the people of Britain have forgotten Jehovah and His promises and warning. The prophet Isaiah touches upon one aspect of our national sin when he proclaims the reproach of the Lord: 'Why spend your money on what is not food, your earnings on what never satisfies? Listen to Me, oh listen, and you shall feed on good, and thrill over the finest fare' (55:2, Moffatt). 'Wherefore do ye spend money for that which is not bread? and your labour for that which satisfieth not?' (A.V.) In view of the vast sums spent on gambling, on entertainment and on narcotics and stimulants, these are questions which the British people might well ask themselves today.

A Hole in Your Pocket!

God's message through the prophet Isaiah is a challenge to us in our present dilemma: 'Hearken to Me, come to Me, listen and you shall revive' (55:3, Moffatt). No one will deny that the British people need to be revived today—morally, materially and, above all, spiritually.

A striking parallel may be observed between the position at the time of the prophet Haggai and our present predicament. A people who had experienced God's deliverance had said in effect: 'Let us first build up a material civilization; there will be plenty of time to rebuild the Temple when we have regained prosperity.' In other words, they had decided that their worldly well-being should have priority over religion. 'Consider your ways,' said God through His prophet, who proceeds to record the troubles which follow their wrong choice: food shortage, insufficient clothing, a money crisis and labour difficulties. One of the most acute problems today is the inflationary spiral because of which workers find that in spite of increased wages they can buy less. Note the words of Haggai and how appropriate they are to the present situation: 'He that earneth wages earneth wages to put it into a bag with holes' (1:6).

The Secret of National Greatness. . .

The solution of the problem of providing an adequate standard of living and freedom from want, which is the rightful heritage of all, is not to be found in any politico-economic theory, but in following the way of life enjoined by Christ when He preached the good news of the Kingdom of God. The people of Britain, who have been trying to build a secular new order in which God is completely left out, are discovering this to their cost, and it is now being realized that the problems facing the nation are beyond human solution, and that the time has come when God's will must be sought. The eternal principles of righteousness—enshrined in the Law of the Lord as given to Moses and ratified by Christ in the Sermon on the Mount—constitute God's will for His people. In them and in them alone is to be found the secret of national well-being and prosperity.

The Divine Law was ordained 'to the end that there be no poor among you' (*Deuteronomy* 15:4, margin), and in the widest sense this means neither poverty in money nor poverty in goods. In an era of potential abundance between the two great wars there was lack of purchasing power accompanied by under-consumption and mass unemployment, with all the poverty and abject misery which such a condition brings in its train. Since the close of the last war there has been a surplus of purchasing power, but at the same time under-production and scarcity with consequent poverty of the necessities of life. Now the cycle appears to be beginning all over again. Both forms of poverty result from infringement of the Divine Law which embodies the principles governing the righteous organization of wealth and work.

... and of Prosperity

A fact to be remembered is that whilst the economic system outlined in the Bible is concerned with material things it rests upon the righteousness of God and upon the right relationship of man with God. Speaking to the people of their material needs Christ emphasized this point when He declared: 'Seek ye first the kingdom of God, and His righteousness; and all these things shall be added unto you' (*Matthew* 6:33). Therein lies the secret of national prosperity: social security and abundance for all will follow righteousness, but they will not, as some would have us believe, beget righteousness.

The eternal principles of righteousness are set forth in the Ten Commandments. These ensure first the right relationship between man and God. The cardinal truth which is lost to the majority of politicians and to the great masses of the people, resulting in much confusion and muddled thinking, is that right relationship between man and man can only be established when a right relationship between man and God has been established. Christ plainly inferred this when He summed up the Commandments thus: 'Thou shalt love the Lord thy God with all thy heart, and with all thy soul, and with all thy mind. This is the first and great commandment. And the second is like unto it, Thou shalt love thy neighbour as thyself' (*Matthew* 22:37-39).

This love of neighbour was expressed in the words of Christ as quoted by St. Paul: 'It is more blessed to give than to receive' (*Acts* 20:35). If this principle were practised the nation would form a contributive society in which people would be more keen to give than to get, more eager to serve than to gain. The more they gave the greater would be their contribution to the common weal, and the greater would be their share in the prosperity of the Commonwealth. At present the reverse is the case. It is not how much we can give but how much we can gain. If all were truly giving of their best, and the attitude were not how much more can we earn, but how much more can we produce, production would soar, prices would fall and even the poorest would be able to buy sufficient to meet all his needs—thus the vicious circle of inflation would be broken.

The moral decline which has been continuing for many decades has now become an accepted feature of the life of the nation. It is not without reason that in the *Daily Graphic* 'Candidus' deplored the fact that today most people 'can hardly tell right from wrong.' This decline is not confined to Britain: it also afflicts the other Anglo-Saxon nations, as is well illustrated in a speech by ex-President Herbert Hoover who, referring to what he calls 'the flight from honour,' said that the United States is experiencing 'a cancerous growth of moral dishonesty in public life.'

The Old Simple Truths

The British people are passing through the most critical phase in their history. Stripped of much of their material power, beset by unparalleled national problems and under the shadow of the EEC, the position of Britain as a Great Power is in jeopardy. 'Candidus' certainly went to the heart of the matter when he pointed out the urgent need to 'proclaim anew the old simple truths that alone make a nation great.' One such truth is the ancient promise:

'If thou shalt hearken diligently unto the voice of the Lord thy God, to observe and to do all His commandments', He 'will set thee on high above all nations of the earth . . . all people of the earth shall see that thou art called by the name of the Lord; and they shall be afraid of thee. And the Lord shall make thee plenteous in goods, in the fruit of thy body, and in the fruit of thy cattle, and in the fruit of thy ground. . . . The Lord shall. . . . bless all the work of thine hand: and thou shalt lend unto many nations, and thou shalt not borrow. And the Lord shall make thee the head, and not the tail; and thou shalt be above only, and thou shalt not be beneath; if that thou hearken unto the commandments of the Lord thy God' (*Deuteronomy* 28:1-13).

What profound lessons the Bible has to teach not only Britain but all the English-speaking nations and their leaders concerning the problems with which they are at present faced.

Incident upon incident demonstrates that during critical episodes in the history of the British people, especially when they have turned to Him and sought His aid, God has intervened on their behalf. Past monarchs, leaders of the Church, statesmen and politicians have testified to their belief that we have been preserved for a purpose. The mission of the peoples of the British Commonwealth and the United States, and also of the kindred peoples on the shores of North-West Europe, is that of God's servants: to quote again Dr. Temple, God 'has a purpose for us to serve in the preparation of His perfect Kingdom.' The fashion in which Britain serves that purpose depends upon national repentance. Yet, despite welcome signs here and there of revival, despite an occasional crowded church where there is a faithful preacher who proclaims the Gospel with power and conviction, Britain continues along the false road of sterile materialism which can only lead to increasing chaos and eventual humiliation.

The call must go forth for national repentance in the clear understanding that the repentance of the nation can only come about as the result of the repentance of individuals making up the nation, for all share the responsibility for national sins and shortcomings. As individuals we must take the first step and heed the challenge. 'The kingdom of God is at hand: repent ye, and believe the gospel.'

The publishers wish to make grateful acknowledgment to the following authors and publishers for the use of extracts from their various works:

A Short History of the English People (1891 Edition), by John Richard Green (Macmillan).

On the Side of the Angels by Harold Begbie (Hodder & Stoughton).

The Defence of London, 1915-1918 by Lt.-Col. Sir A. Rawlinson, C.M.G., C.B.E., D.S.O. (Melrose).

The Struggle for Europe by Chester Wilmot (Collins).

World War II by Winston S. Churchill, O.M. (Cassell).

Hitler's Strategy by F. H. Hinsley (Cambridge University Press).

A Very Present Help by Lt.-Gen. Sir Wm. Dobbie, G.C.M.G., K.C.B., D.S.O. (Marshall, Morgan & Scott).

A Sailor's Odyssey by Admiral of the Fleet, Viscount Cunningham of Hyndhope, K.T., G.C.B., O.M., D.S.O. (Hutchinson).

Pipeline to Battle by Major Peter W. Rainier (Heinemann).

The History of UNRRA (The Columbia University Press).

The Mediterranean Fleet; The Eighth Army; Tunisia (H.M. Stationery Office).

Miracles of Prayer Stopped the Terrorist – 'Operation Esther' by Harvey Ward, pub. 1987 by New Leaf Press Inc. PO Box 311, Green Forest, AR 72638, USA (ISBN 0-89221-146-6).

Christ on Trial in Zimbabwe-Rhodesia by Thomas Barlow, pub. 1979 by the Dorothea Mission, PO Box 219, Pretoria 0001, South Africa.

To the Editors of the many magazines and newspapers from which extracts have been taken and to The Imperial War Museum, The National Maritime Museum, 'News Chronicle,' Central Press Photos, Fox Photos, Keystone Press Agency, Picture Post Library, The Associated Equipment Co. Ltd., Southall, The Mary Evans Picture Library and V. J. Lee, *for the use of illustrations.* The photographs of the D-Day windows are copyright Christ Church Portsdown Parochial Church Council. Used by permission. All rights reserved.

'We commend the Gospel of Christ our Saviour, for it alone can effectively mould character, control conduct and solve the problems of men and nations, and thus make life what it should be.

'Faith in Christ the Lord, and loyal obedience to His will as revealed in the Bible, ensures peace of mind and brings satisfaction in service to God and man.'

ANDREW CUNNINGHAM, *Admiral of the Fleet.*
JACK C. TOVEY, *Admiral.*
H. R. ALEXANDER, *General.*
B. PAGET, *General.*
E.L. GEORGE, *Air Marshal.*

The above statement was signed by these Commanders-in-Chief of the Royal Navy, Army and Royal Air Force early in World War II as a foreword to one of the Gospels distributed to members of the Forces.

I Desire Solemnly to call my People to prayer and dedication. We are not unmindful of our own shortcomings, past and present. We shall ask not that God may do our will, but that we may be enabled to do the will of God; and we dare to believe that God has used our Nation and Empire as an instrument for fulfilling His high purpose.

His Majesty's Call to Prayer to the Nation, June 6th, 1944.

Days of Prayer

There were seven Days of Prayer called by King George VI at these crucial times. The nation trusted God and remained united in adversity never once contemplating defeat.

1. *Dunkirk*

Crowds flocked to church to pray for the men stranded on the beaches and Churchill ordered every available sea-going vessel across the Channel, hoping to snatch 30,000 back. A miracle occurred as the water became as calm as a millpond, enabling even the smallest crafts to set sail, and a heavy storm grounded the Luftwaffe. Hitler then inexplicably halted his advance and within 10 days more than 335,000 Allied military personnel were rescued.

2 & 3. *Battle of Britain*

The German objective was to destroy the RAF and its airfields.

a) A Day of Prayer was called at the height of the Battle on Sunday 11 August, 1940, and the King made an appeal to all young people to pray especially for the equally young pilots. Many responded, resulting in abandoned tennis courts and playing fields. During the following week Spitfires and Hurricanes shot down 180 Nazi bombers.

b) On 30 August, 1940, 800 enemy aircraft filled the skies intending to destroy key RAF airfields. By 6 September the situation was dire and defeat in the air seemed inevitable. The King therefore called another Day of Prayer on 8 September when churches were full to bursting. That week 185 German planes were shot down and Goering gave up his assault. By 15 September Churchill was able to declare victory in the air.

4. *Planned Invasion of Britain*

The next Day of Prayer was called by the King on 23 March, 1941, during a period of heavy bombing in London. He was unaware it was the actual date planned by Hitler for the invasion! German ships were soon blown off course and the Fuehrer changed his entire plans, switching instead to an invasion of Russia.

5. *North Africa*

The fifth Day of Prayer was called in September 1942 when the British Eighth Army had been driven back to the borders of Egypt by Rommel's Afrika Korps. General Montgomery was appointed as the Eighth Army Commander and led British forces to the significant victory at El Alamein when Rommel was on leave and enemy fuel supplies from Rome failed to arrive on time. The battle was a turning point in the war.

6. *Italy defeated*
A Day of Prayer was called on 3 September, 1943, the fourth anniversary of the declaration of war on Germany. Italy surrendered to the Allies within 24 hours and Mussolini was assassinated.

7. *D-Day and beyond*
The seventh Day of Prayer was called in Spring 1944, for all military personnel. The poor weather hindering the D-Day offensive suddenly relented and fine weather on 6 June allowed the Normandy invasion of France and Europe to begin, during which time far fewer lives than expected were lost.

With acknowledgement to **E JOHN METCALFE**
This England Winter 2010